THE FULLY REVEALED CHRIST

The Fully Revealed Christ

TONY MEDLEY

MEDLEY

Title: *The Fully Revealed Christ: A New Testament Survey Guide*
Author: Dr. Tony E. Medley, Sr.

Published by Medley Publishing Group
Printed in the United States of America

ISBN (Paperback): 979-8-9940033-7-4
ISBN (eBook): 979-8-9940033-8-1

Unless otherwise indicated, Scripture quotations are taken from the Holy
Bible. All emphasis within Scripture quotations (including italics, bold
type, or capitalization) has been added by the author for instructional and
academic clarity.

This publication is intended for use in **Bible colleges, seminaries, ac-
credited Christian institutions, church education programs, and
guided independent study**. It is designed to support structured course-
work, theological education, and spiritual formation in alignment with in-
stitutional learning objectives.

This book is not intended to replace personal study of Scripture, pastoral
oversight, or formal theological instruction, but to serve as a **supplemen-
tal academic and instructional resource** that encourages rigorous en-
gagement with the Word of God.

CONTENTS

~~

Preface

The New Testament is not simply a collection of writings—it is the Spirit-breathed unveiling of Jesus Christ in His fullness. The Gospels reveal Him as the incarnate Son; Acts demonstrates His power through the Church; the Epistles declare His doctrine and guidance; and Revelation exalts Him as the Lamb who reigns forever.

This book was born out of a conviction that students of the Word need a guide that is both expository and practical, a resource that not only outlines the message of each New Testament book but also brings Christ's presence alive in every chapter. My aim is not to impress with scholarship but to ignite a passion for Scripture that transforms life.

I pray that as you read, your eyes will be opened afresh to behold Christ in His glory, your heart stirred to love Him more deeply, and your will strengthened to serve Him more faithfully.

Acknowledgements

No work of this scope is accomplished in isolation. I first give glory to God the Father, who revealed His Son, and to the Holy Spirit, who breathes life into the pages of Scripture.

I extend gratitude to the students of the Word of God whose hunger for truth inspired me to develop this resource. Your questions, insights, and faithfulness sharpened my calling.

To my family, who have stood beside me with patience and love, thank you for your sacrifices that allowed this vision to become a reality.

To every pastor, teacher, and believer who longs to see Christ more clearly—I dedicate this book to you. May you find in these pages tools to strengthen your walk and your ministry.

Introduction

The call of discipleship is not to a program but to a Person—Jesus Christ. Yet in an age of noise, confusion, and shifting truths, many believers know of Him without truly knowing Him in the fullness of His Word.

This New Testament Survey Guide is designed for students, ministers, and lay believers who long to see Christ revealed on every page. Each chapter will:

- Introduce the background and purpose of the book.
- Exposit the main themes and truths.
- Highlight how Christ is revealed uniquely in that book.
- Provide reflection questions for growth and application.

The study guide format makes it ready for use in classrooms, Bible studies, and personal devotion. My desire is that it will help you not merely to study about Christ but to experience Christ.

The words of John 20:31 echo as the guiding heartbeat: "But these are written that you may believe that Jesus is the Messiah, the Son of God, and that by believing you may have life in his name."

PART I: THE GOSPELS

Christ Revealed in His Life and Ministry

~ One ~

MATTHEW

As we open the New Testament, we are introduced to the Gospel of Matthew. This is no accident—Matthew intentionally bridges the Old Testament promises with the New Testament fulfillment in Christ. He writes to a Jewish audience, showing them that Jesus is the long-awaited Messiah, the Son of David, the Son of Abraham, the King who brings God's Kingdom to earth.

Matthew's Gospel is sometimes called "the Gospel of the Kingdom." Over and over, he emphasizes that the rule and reign of God has broken into history in the person of Jesus Christ. Yet Matthew also shows that this King came not to overthrow Rome but to conquer sin and death. He is the King who reigns from a cross, and through His resurrection, commissions His disciples to take the gospel to all nations.

Background of Matthew

- Author: Matthew (Levi), a former tax collector turned disciple.
- Date: Approx. AD 60–65.
- Audience: Primarily Jewish believers but also the wider church.
- Purpose: To present Jesus as the promised Messiah and King, fulfilling Old Testament prophecy.

- Key Verse: "All authority in heaven and on earth has been given to me. Therefore go and make disciples of all nations..." (Matthew 28:18–19).

Structure of Matthew

1. The Birth and Early Life of the King (Ch. 1–2)
    - Genealogy and virgin birth.
    - Visit of the Magi.
    - Flight to Egypt.
2. The Message of the King (Ch. 3–7)
    - John the Baptist's ministry.
    - Baptism and temptation of Jesus.
    - Sermon on the Mount.
3. The Works of the King (Ch. 8–10)
    - Miracles, healings, casting out demons.
    - Sending of the Twelve.
4. The Opposition to the King (Ch. 11–13)
    - Rising conflict with religious leaders.
    - Parables of the Kingdom.
5. The Preparation of Disciples (Ch. 14–20)
    - Teachings on discipleship.
    - Predictions of His death.
6. The Passion of the King (Ch. 21–27)
    - Triumphal entry.
    - Betrayal, trial, and crucifixion.
7. The Triumph of the King (Ch. 28)
    - Resurrection.
    - The Great Commission.

Key Themes of Matthew

1. Jesus as Messiah and King – The fulfillment of prophecy.

2. The Kingdom of Heaven – God's rule on earth.
3. Discipleship – Following Jesus under His authority.
4. Conflict with Religious Leaders – True righteousness vs. legalism.
5. The Mission to the Nations – The gospel for all people.

Exposition and Lessons

1. Jesus the Promised King (Ch. 1-2)

Matthew begins with a genealogy proving Jesus' royal lineage as the Son of David. He fulfills prophecy through His virgin birth and His early life events.

Lesson: God keeps His promises. Every detail of Jesus' birth reveals God's faithfulness.

2. The Sermon on the Mount (Ch. 5-7)

Here Jesus lays out the ethics of the Kingdom—calling His disciples to a righteousness that surpasses the Pharisees. He addresses the heart, not just outward actions.

Lesson: Kingdom living means transformed hearts, not external rule-keeping.

3. The Miracles of the King (Ch. 8-10)

Jesus demonstrates His authority over sickness, demons, nature, and death. He then empowers His disciples to share in this ministry.

Lesson: The authority of Christ is real and available for His followers today.

4. Parables of the Kingdom (Ch. 13)

Through parables, Jesus reveals the mystery of the Kingdom: it begins small but grows, it is opposed but unstoppable.

Lesson: God's Kingdom often works quietly and unexpectedly, but it will triumph.

5. The Cross and Resurrection (Ch. 26–28)

Jesus is betrayed, tried, crucified, and raised. The climax of Matthew's Gospel shows the King laying down His life for His people, then rising to commission them to the nations.

Lesson: The Kingdom advances through the cross. Christ's victory comes through sacrifice.

Christ Revealed in Matthew

- Immanuel—God with us (1:23).
- The New Moses, giving the true Law (Ch. 5–7).
- The Suffering Servant (Ch. 26–27).
- The Risen King with all authority (28:18–20).

Memory Verse

Matthew 28:19 – "Therefore go and make disciples of all nations..."

Reflection Questions

1. How does Matthew connect the Old Testament promises with Jesus' life?
2. What is the significance of Jesus being called "Immanuel"?
3. How does the Sermon on the Mount challenge our understanding of righteousness?

4. What do the parables teach about the nature of God's Kingdom?

5. How does the Great Commission apply to you personally?

Final Exhortation

Students, Matthew shows us that Jesus is not simply a historical figure but the living King. He has all authority in heaven and on earth, and He calls us to follow Him, learn from Him, and proclaim His Kingdom.

The question for each of us is this: Will we bow to Him as King? If so, our lives must be marked by obedience, humility, and mission. Let Matthew's Gospel ignite your passion to live as disciples who make disciples, until every nation has heard that Christ is King.

~ Two ~

MARK

The Gospel of Mark is the shortest of the four Gospels, but it is full of urgency and power. Mark wastes no time on long introductions—he launches straight into the action: "The beginning of the good news about Jesus the Messiah, the Son of God" (Mark 1:1).

Where Matthew emphasizes Jesus as King, Mark portrays Him as the Servant of the Lord. This Gospel shows Jesus constantly at work—healing, teaching, casting out demons, and serving. Mark's favorite word is "immediately," reminding us that the Kingdom of God demands a response now.

Yet this Servant is also the Suffering Servant. The heart of Mark's Gospel is found in 10:45: "For even the Son of Man did not come to be served, but to serve, and to give his life as a ransom for many."

Mark teaches us that following Jesus is not about power or prestige—it is about service, sacrifice, and cross-shaped discipleship.

Background of Mark

- Author: John Mark, companion of Peter and Paul. His Gospel reflects Peter's eyewitness testimony.
- Date: ~AD 55–65, likely written in Rome.
- Audience: Roman believers, especially Gentiles unfamiliar with Jewish customs.

- Purpose: To present Jesus as the Servant-Savior and call believers to faithful discipleship.
- Key Verse: "For even the Son of Man did not come to be served, but to serve, and to give his life as a ransom for many." (Mark 10:45)

Structure of Mark

1. The Authority of the Servant (Ch. 1–8)
    - Jesus' baptism and temptation.
    - Healings, miracles, exorcisms.
    - Growing crowds and conflict.
2. The Identity of the Servant (Ch. 8–10)
    - Peter's confession: "You are the Messiah."
    - First predictions of the cross.
    - Teaching on true discipleship.
3. The Mission of the Servant (Ch. 11–16)
    - Triumphal entry.
    - Betrayal, crucifixion, and resurrection.

Key Themes of Mark

1. Jesus the Servant – He ministers with compassion and power.
2. The Authority of Christ – Over demons, disease, and nature.
3. The Cross – Central to His mission.
4. Urgency of the Gospel – The time is now to respond.
5. Discipleship – Following Jesus means carrying the cross.

Exposition and Lessons

1. The Servant at Work (Ch. 1–3)

Mark shows Jesus preaching, healing, and casting out demons with authority. Crowds flock to Him, but opposition also rises.

Lesson: The gospel confronts both brokenness and spiritual darkness with God's power.

2. Parables and Power (Ch. 4–6)

Jesus teaches the parable of the sower, calms the storm, casts out Legion, and feeds the five thousand. His authority is unmatched.

Lesson: Nothing is beyond Christ's power—He commands nature, demons, and disease.

3. The Turning Point (Ch. 8)

Peter confesses Jesus as the Messiah. But Jesus immediately explains that the Messiah must suffer, be rejected, and die. The disciples struggle to understand.

Lesson: To follow Christ is to accept the way of the cross.

4. Teaching on Discipleship (Ch. 9–10)

Jesus calls His followers to humility, childlike faith, and servant leadership. He declares: "The first will be last, and the last first."

Lesson: True greatness is measured by service, not status.

5. The Passion Narrative (Ch. 11–16)

Mark devotes a third of his Gospel to the final week of Jesus' life. The King enters Jerusalem, is betrayed, tried, crucified, and then raised in glory.

Lesson: The cross is not a detour but the destination of Christ's mission.

Christ Revealed in Mark

- The Servant who ministers with compassion (1:41).
- The Teacher with authority (1:22).
- The Miracle-worker with power over creation (4:39).
- The Suffering Servant who gives His life as ransom (10:45).
- The Risen Lord who conquers death (16:6).

Memory Verse

Mark 10:45 – "For even the Son of Man did not come to be served, but to serve, and to give his life as a ransom for many."

Reflection Questions

1. Why is it significant that Mark highlights Jesus as a Servant?
2. How do Jesus' miracles demonstrate His authority?
3. Why did Peter struggle to accept a suffering Messiah?
4. How does Mark challenge our understanding of discipleship?
5. What does Mark's urgency ("immediately") teach us about responding to the gospel?

Final Exhortation

Students, Mark's Gospel calls us to recognize Jesus not only as Lord but as Servant. He shows us that greatness in God's Kingdom is found not in being served but in serving.

Mark also calls us to urgent discipleship. There is no time to delay—the Kingdom of God is here. Will you take up your cross and follow Him? Will you serve as He served, even to the point of sacrifice?

Let Mark inspire you to a life of humble service, urgent mission, and faithful obedience to Christ the Servant-King.

~ Three ~

LUKE

The Gospel of Luke presents Jesus as the Son of Man, the Savior who identifies with humanity in all its weakness and need. Luke, a physician and companion of Paul, gives us the most detailed and orderly account of Jesus' life. He writes not only as a historian but as a pastor, showing us that the gospel is for all people—Jews, Gentiles, men, women, rich, poor, outcast, and marginalized.

Luke emphasizes Jesus' compassion for the broken, His ministry to the poor, His concern for women and children, and His love for sinners. Above all, Luke reveals that Jesus came "to seek and to save the lost" (Luke 19:10).

Background of Luke

- Author: Luke, the beloved physician, companion of Paul.
- Date: ~AD 60–62.
- Audience: Addressed to Theophilus, but written for a broad Gentile audience.
- Purpose: To provide an orderly account so that believers may know the certainty of what they have been taught (Luke 1:4).
- Key Verse: "For the Son of Man came to seek and to save the lost." (Luke 19:10)

Structure of Luke

1. Prologue and Birth Narratives (Ch. 1–2)
   - Announcements to Zechariah and Mary.
   - Births of John the Baptist and Jesus.
   - Angels, shepherds, and Simeon's prophecy.
2. Preparation for Ministry (Ch. 3–4)
   - Baptism, genealogy, and temptation of Jesus.
3. Ministry in Galilee (Ch. 4–9)
   - Teachings, miracles, calling of disciples.
   - Transfiguration.
4. Journey to Jerusalem (Ch. 9–19)
   - Parables of mercy and discipleship.
   - Encounters with the marginalized.
   - Zacchaeus and the mission statement (19:10).
5. Passion, Death, and Resurrection (Ch. 19–24)
   - Triumphal entry, Last Supper, crucifixion.
   - Resurrection and Emmaus Road appearance.

Key Themes of Luke

1. Jesus the Son of Man – Fully God, fully human, identifying with us.
2. Universal Salvation – The gospel is for all nations and all classes.
3. Compassion for the Marginalized – Outcasts, women, children, sinners.
4. The Role of the Holy Spirit – From Jesus' birth to the church's mission.
5. Prayer and Joy – Luke highlights prayer more than any Gospel writer.

Exposition and Lessons

1. A Savior for All People (Ch. 1-2)

The angel declares: "I bring you good news that will cause great joy for all the people" (2:10). Luke's birth narratives highlight the humble and the overlooked—Mary, shepherds, Simeon, and Anna.

Lesson: God's kingdom values the humble and lifts up the lowly.

2. Ministry to the Marginalized (Ch. 4-7)

Jesus proclaims in Nazareth: "The Spirit of the Lord is on me... He has anointed me to proclaim good news to the poor" (4:18). He heals lepers, forgives sinners, and welcomes the outcast.

Lesson: No one is beyond the reach of Christ's compassion.

3. Parables of Mercy (Ch. 10-18)

Luke uniquely includes parables like the Good Samaritan, the Prodigal Son, and the Rich Man and Lazarus. These stories reveal God's mercy and call for radical compassion.

Lesson: True discipleship shows mercy, forgiveness, and generosity.

4. The Mission Statement (Ch. 19:10)

In Zacchaeus' story, Jesus declares His purpose: "For the Son of Man came to seek and to save the lost."

Lesson: Christ's mission—and ours—is to seek the lost with the gospel.

5. *The Cross and Resurrection (Ch. 22–24)*

Luke emphasizes Jesus' innocence (Pilate and Herod declare Him not guilty). At the cross, the repentant thief is promised paradise. The risen Lord appears on the Emmaus Road, opening the Scriptures about Himself.

Lesson: Salvation is available to all who repent and believe, no matter their past.

Christ Revealed in Luke

- The Son of Man who identifies with humanity (3:23–38).
- The compassionate Savior of the outcast (7:36–50).
- The Good Samaritan who rescues us (10:25–37).
- The Prodigal's Father who welcomes us home (15:11–32).
- The Redeemer who seeks and saves the lost (19:10).
- The Risen Lord who opens the Scriptures (24:27).

Memory Verse

Luke 19:10 – "For the Son of Man came to seek and to save the lost."

Reflection Questions

1. Why does Luke emphasize that the gospel is for all people?
2. How do Jesus' parables in Luke highlight God's mercy?
3. What does the story of Zacchaeus teach us about salvation?
4. How does Luke's focus on the marginalized challenge the church today?
5. What does it mean that Jesus is the "Son of Man"?

Final Exhortation

Students, Luke's Gospel reminds us that Jesus is both fully divine and fully human—the Son of God and the Son of Man. He came not for the righteous but for sinners, not for the powerful but for the powerless.

If you have ever felt overlooked, Luke shows you that Christ sees you. If you have ever felt unworthy, Luke shows you that Christ welcomes you. And if you have ever wondered about your purpose, Luke makes it clear: as Christ came to seek and save the lost, so must we.

Let Luke ignite your joy, deepen your compassion, and call you into Christ's mission.

~ Four ~

JOHN

The Gospel of John is unlike the other three Gospels. Matthew, Mark, and Luke (the Synoptics) give us a portrait of Jesus' ministry through His parables, miracles, and travels. But John takes us deeper into the heart of Christ—His identity as the eternal Son of God.

John's purpose is crystal clear: "But these are written that you may believe that Jesus is the Messiah, the Son of God, and that by believing you may have life in his name" (John 20:31).

John presents Jesus as the Word made flesh (1:14), the Lamb of God who takes away the sin of the world (1:29), the Light of the world (8:12), the Good Shepherd (10:11), the Resurrection and the Life (11:25), and the True Vine (15:5). His Gospel calls us not just to know about Jesus but to believe in Him and have eternal life.

Background of John

- Author: John the Apostle, "the disciple whom Jesus loved."
- Date: ~AD 85–95, the last of the four Gospels written.
- Audience: Both Jews and Gentiles, with a universal scope.
- Purpose: To reveal Jesus as the eternal Son of God and bring people to saving faith.
- Key Verse: "But these are written that you may believe that Jesus is the Messiah, the Son of God, and that by believing you may have life in his name." (John 20:31)

Structure of John

1. The Prologue (Ch. 1:1–18)
   ◦ The Word made flesh.
2. The Book of Signs (Ch. 1:19–12:50)
   ◦ Seven signs (miracles) revealing Christ's glory.
3. The Book of Glory (Ch. 13–20)
   ◦ Last Supper, crucifixion, resurrection.
4. The Epilogue (Ch. 21)
   ◦ Jesus restores Peter and commissions His disciples.

Key Themes of John

1. Jesus the Son of God – Eternal, divine, one with the Father.
2. Eternal Life Through Faith – Believing in Him brings life.
3. Signs and Testimony – Miracles that reveal His glory.
4. The "I AM" Sayings – Jesus' divine self-revelation.
5. Love and Discipleship – The new commandment to love as He loved.

Exposition and Lessons

1. The Word Made Flesh (Ch. 1:1-18)

John begins with eternity: "In the beginning was the Word, and the Word was with God, and the Word was God." Jesus is God Himself, yet He became flesh to dwell among us.

Lesson: The incarnation is the ultimate revelation of God's love.

2. The Seven Signs (Ch. 2-11)

John records seven miracles, each pointing to Christ's divine identity:

1. Water into wine (Ch. 2).
2. Healing the nobleman's son (Ch. 4).
3. Healing the paralytic (Ch. 5).
4. Feeding the five thousand (Ch. 6).
5. Walking on water (Ch. 6).
6. Healing the man born blind (Ch. 9).
7. Raising Lazarus from the dead (Ch. 11).

Lesson: These signs are not just wonders—they reveal Christ's power to transform, heal, provide, and give life.

3. The "I AM" Sayings (Ch. 6–15)

Jesus makes seven "I AM" declarations, echoing God's name in Exodus 3:14:

- I am the Bread of Life (6:35).
- I am the Light of the World (8:12).
- I am the Gate (10:9).
- I am the Good Shepherd (10:11).
- I am the Resurrection and the Life (11:25).
- I am the Way, the Truth, and the Life (14:6).
- I am the True Vine (15:5).

Lesson: Jesus is everything we need for salvation, guidance, and eternal life.

4. The Upper Room Discourse (Ch. 13–17)

On the night before His crucifixion, Jesus washes His disciples' feet, gives the new commandment of love, promises the Holy Spirit, and prays for His followers.

Lesson: True discipleship is marked by love, service, and the Spirit's power.

5. The Cross and Resurrection (Ch. 18–20)

John presents the cross not as defeat but as glory—Jesus lifted up to draw all people to Himself (12:32). The resurrection is the ultimate sign, proving He is the Son of God and giver of life.

Lesson: Eternal life is secured through Christ's death and resurrection.

6. The Epilogue (Ch. 21)

The risen Jesus restores Peter, showing that failure is not final. He commissions His disciples to follow Him and feed His sheep.

Lesson: Christ restores and recommissions us after failure.

Christ Revealed in John

- The Word made flesh (1:14).
- The Lamb of God (1:29).
- The Great "I AM."
- The Good Shepherd (10:11).
- The Resurrection and the Life (11:25).
- The Way, Truth, and Life (14:6).
- The Risen Lord (20:28).

Memory Verse

John 20:31 – "But these are written that you may believe that Jesus is the Messiah, the Son of God, and that by believing you may have life in his name."

Reflection Questions

1. How does John emphasize the divinity of Christ differently than the Synoptic Gospels?
2. What do the seven signs reveal about Jesus' power and mission?
3. Which "I AM" saying speaks most to your life right now, and why?
4. What does John teach us about discipleship in the Upper Room?
5. How does the resurrection shape our understanding of eternal life?

Final Exhortation

Students, John's Gospel is written with one purpose: that you may believe and have life in Christ. It calls you to see Jesus not only as a teacher or prophet but as the eternal Son of God, the Word made flesh, the Lamb who died for your sins, and the Lord who rose again.

To study John is to be confronted with the most important decision of life: Will you believe? For John assures us that to believe in Him is to pass from death to life, from darkness to light, from despair to joy.

Let John's Gospel stir your faith, strengthen your assurance, and send you into the world proclaiming, "Jesus is Lord!"

PART II: ACTS

Christ at Work Through His Church

~ Five ~

ACTS

The book of Acts is the bridge between the Gospels and the Epistles. It records the birth of the church and the unstoppable advance of the gospel through the power of the Holy Spirit.

Luke, the author of the Gospel of Luke, continues his account here, showing how the risen Christ continues His work through His Spirit-filled disciples. What Jesus began in His earthly ministry, He now continues through His body, the church.

The theme of Acts can be summarized in one verse: "But you will receive power when the Holy Spirit comes on you; and you will be my witnesses in Jerusalem, and in all Judea and Samaria, and to the ends of the earth." (Acts 1:8).

Acts is not just ancient history—it is the pattern for the church today. We are still called to be Spirit-empowered witnesses to the ends of the earth.

Background of Acts

- Author: Luke, physician and companion of Paul.
- Date: ~AD 62.
- Audience: Addressed to Theophilus; intended for all believers.
- Purpose: To trace the spread of the gospel from Jerusalem to Rome through the work of the Spirit.
- Key Verse: Acts 1:8.

Structure of Acts

1. The Church Empowered (Ch. 1–7)
    ◦ Ascension and Pentecost.
    ◦ Growth and opposition in Jerusalem.
2. The Church Scattered (Ch. 8–12)
    ◦ Persecution spreads the gospel.
    ◦ Conversion of Saul.
    ◦ Peter opens the door to Gentiles.
3. The Church Sent (Ch. 13–28)
    ◦ Paul's missionary journeys.
    ◦ The gospel reaches Rome.

Key Themes of Acts

1. The Holy Spirit Empowers – The Spirit is the main actor in Acts.
2. The Gospel for All Nations – From Jerusalem to the ends of the earth.
3. The Church as Witness – Called to proclaim Christ boldly.
4. Suffering and Mission – Persecution spreads the gospel.
5. Unity in Diversity – Jews and Gentiles united in Christ.

Exposition and Lessons

1. The Ascension and Promise (Ch. 1)

Jesus ascends to heaven, promising the Holy Spirit. The disciples are called to wait until they are clothed with power.

Lesson: Ministry must be Spirit-empowered, not self-driven.

2. Pentecost (Ch. 2)

The Spirit is poured out; Peter preaches, and three thousand are saved. The church is born, marked by teaching, fellowship, breaking bread, and prayer.

Lesson: The Spirit empowers the church for mission and community.

3. Bold Witness in Jerusalem (Ch. 3–7)

The apostles perform miracles and proclaim Christ. Opposition grows, but the church thrives. Stephen becomes the first martyr, declaring Christ even in death.

Lesson: The gospel advances through boldness, even in persecution.

4. The Gospel Spreads to Samaria and Beyond (Ch. 8–12)

Philip preaches in Samaria, the Ethiopian eunuch is converted, and Saul (Paul) encounters the risen Christ. Peter preaches to Cornelius, proving the gospel is for Gentiles too.

Lesson: The gospel knows no boundaries—racial, social, or geographic.

5. Paul's Missionary Journeys (Ch. 13–21)

Paul and Barnabas set out to plant churches across Asia Minor and Greece. Despite persecution, the gospel flourishes.

Lesson: God uses ordinary people to spread His extraordinary message.

6. The Gospel Reaches Rome (Ch. 21–28)

Paul is arrested, tried, and sent to Rome. The book ends with Paul proclaiming the kingdom of God under house arrest.

Lesson: God's mission cannot be stopped—chains cannot bind the gospel.

Christ Revealed in Acts

- The Ascended Lord who sends the Spirit (1:9–11).
- The Risen Savior proclaimed by the apostles (2:32–33).
- The Cornerstone rejected by men but exalted by God (4:11).
- The Light to the Gentiles (13:47).
- The Lord of all who calls people from every nation (10:34–35).

Memory Verse

Acts 1:8 – "But you will receive power when the Holy Spirit comes on you; and you will be my witnesses in Jerusalem, and in all Judea and Samaria, and to the ends of the earth."

Reflection Questions

1. How does Acts show the church's dependence on the Holy Spirit?
2. What does Pentecost teach us about the mission of the church?
3. How does persecution advance rather than hinder the gospel?
4. What lessons do Paul's missionary journeys teach us about ministry today?
5. How does Acts challenge you personally to be a witness?

Final Exhortation

Students, Acts reminds us that the story of the church is the story of God's Spirit working through His people. The book does not truly end—it continues today through us.

You are called to be a witness—to your family, your community, your nation, and the world. The same Spirit who empowered Peter, Stephen, Philip, and Paul dwells in you.

So I urge you: live boldly, serve faithfully, and proclaim Christ courageously. For the mission of Acts is still the mission of the church today—to carry the good news of Jesus to the ends of the earth.

PART III: THE LETTERS OF PAUL

Christ in Doctrine and Discipleship

~ Six ~

ROMANS

The book of Romans stands as Paul's greatest theological masterpiece. Written to the church in Rome, a community he had not yet visited, Romans lays out the most systematic presentation of the gospel in all of Scripture.

Paul reveals that the righteousness of God is made available not through works, law, or human effort, but through faith in Jesus Christ. He shows us the universal problem of sin, the sufficiency of Christ's sacrifice, the new life in the Spirit, and the practical outworking of the gospel in daily life.

Romans has been called the "Constitution of Christianity," and for good reason. From Augustine to Martin Luther to John Wesley, this book has ignited spiritual awakenings throughout history. And today, it continues to transform lives with the message: "The righteous will live by faith." (Romans 1:17).

Background of Romans

- Author: Paul the Apostle.
- Date: ~AD 57, written from Corinth.
- Audience: The church in Rome, composed of both Jews and Gentiles.
- Purpose: To explain the gospel clearly, unite believers, and prepare for Paul's mission to Spain.

• Key Verse: "For in the gospel the righteousness of God is re-vealed—a righteousness that is by faith from first to last, just as it is written: 'The righteous will live by faith.'" (Romans 1:17).

Structure of Romans

1. The Need for Righteousness (Ch. 1–3)
    ◦ All have sinned and fall short.
2. The Gift of Righteousness (Ch. 4–5)
    ◦ Justification by faith.
3. The Power of Righteousness (Ch. 6–8)
    ◦ Freedom from sin, life in the Spirit.
4. God's Plan for Israel (Ch. 9–11)
    ◦ God's sovereignty in salvation.
5. The Practice of Righteousness (Ch. 12–16)
    ◦ Living out the gospel in community and mission.

Key Themes of Romans

1. The Universal Problem of Sin – All are guilty before God.
2. Justification by Faith – Salvation is by grace alone through faith alone.
3. New Life in the Spirit – Believers are free from condemnation.
4. God's Sovereign Plan – His purposes for Jews and Gentiles.
5. Practical Christianity – The gospel transforms daily life.

Exposition and Lessons

1. The Need for Righteousness (Ch. 1–3)

Paul begins with the bad news: Gentiles are guilty of rejecting God (Ch. 1), Jews are guilty of hypocrisy (Ch. 2), and ultimately, "there is no one righteous, not even one" (3:10).

Lesson: Every person stands in need of God's grace—no exceptions.

2. Justification by Faith (Ch. 4–5)

Paul points to Abraham as the model: he was justified by faith, not works. Through Christ's sacrifice, we are declared righteous and have peace with God (5:1).

Lesson: Salvation is a gift received by faith, not earned by performance.

3. New Life in Christ (Ch. 6–8)

Paul explains that believers are united with Christ in His death and resurrection. Sin no longer reigns. Life in the Spirit brings freedom from condemnation (8:1) and assurance of God's love (8:38–39).

Lesson: The Christian life is lived in the power of the Spirit, not in human strength.

4. God's Sovereignty and Israel (Ch. 9–11)

Paul wrestles with Israel's unbelief, affirming God's sovereign choice and His ultimate plan to include both Jews and Gentiles in salvation.

Lesson: God's purposes never fail—His mercy extends to all.

5. Living Out the Gospel (Ch. 12-16)

The final chapters give practical instructions: offer your body as a living sacrifice (12:1), love sincerely, submit to authorities, and pursue unity in the church.

Lesson: The gospel transforms not only what we believe but how we live.

Christ Revealed in Romans

- The Righteousness of God (1:17).
- The Second Adam (5:12–21).
- The Deliverer from sin and death (7:24–25).
- The Condemned One, so we are not condemned (8:1).
- The Intercessor at God's right hand (8:34).
- The Root of Jesse who brings salvation to Jews and Gentiles (15:12).

Memory Verse

Romans 1:17 – "The righteous will live by faith."

Reflection Questions

1. How does Romans show that all people—Jew and Gentile—need salvation?
2. What does it mean to be "justified by faith"?
3. How does Romans 8 encourage believers in their daily struggles?
4. What do chapters 9–11 teach us about God's sovereignty?
5. How does Romans challenge us to live out the gospel practically?

Final Exhortation

Students, Romans takes us to the very heart of the gospel. It humbles us by exposing our sin, exalts Christ by showing His sufficiency, and transforms us by the power of the Spirit.

The message of Romans is clear: we are saved by grace, through faith, in Christ alone. This truth sets us free, assures us of God's love, and compels us to live for His glory.

As you study Romans, let it not remain theory—let it change you. Offer your life as a living sacrifice, renewed by the gospel, and join Paul in proclaiming Christ to the nations.

~ Seven ~

1 CORINTHIANS

The book of 1 Corinthians is Paul's pastoral letter to a troubled church. The believers in Corinth were gifted, enthusiastic, and full of potential—but they were also divided, immature, and influenced by the immorality of their culture.

Paul writes to correct their errors, call them back to holiness, and show them that the cross of Christ is the true measure of wisdom and power. He deals with issues of division, pride, immorality, lawsuits, marriage, worship, spiritual gifts, and resurrection.

Through it all, Paul emphasizes that Jesus Christ is the foundation of the church, and love is the greatest expression of Christian maturity.

Background of 1 Corinthians

- Author: Paul the Apostle.
- Date: ~AD 55, written from Ephesus.
- Audience: The church in Corinth, a wealthy but immoral city.
- Purpose: To correct divisions and sins, answer questions, and call believers to unity in Christ.
- Key Verse: "For I resolved to know nothing while I was with you except Jesus Christ and him crucified." (1 Corinthians 2:2).

Structure of 1 Corinthians

1. Divisions in the Church (Ch. 1–4)
    ◦ The cross vs. human wisdom.
    ◦ Unity in Christ.
2. Discipline in the Church (Ch. 5–6)
    ◦ Immorality and lawsuits.
3. Marriage and Singleness (Ch. 7)
    ◦ Guidance for relationships.
4. Liberty and Responsibility (Ch. 8–10)
    ◦ Food offered to idols.
    ◦ Living for God's glory.
5. Worship and Order (Ch. 11–14)
    ◦ The Lord's Supper.
    ◦ Spiritual gifts and love.
6. The Resurrection (Ch. 15)
    ◦ Christ's resurrection and ours.
7. Final Instructions (Ch. 16)
    ◦ Giving, travel plans, greetings.

Key Themes of 1 Corinthians

1. Christ the Foundation – All ministry is built on Him.
2. The Cross is True Wisdom – God's power is revealed in weakness.
3. Unity in the Church – Division dishonors Christ.
4. Holiness in Lifestyle – Believers must live differently from the world.
5. Love Above All – Spiritual gifts without love are nothing.
6. The Hope of Resurrection – Christ's victory guarantees ours.

Exposition and Lessons

1. Divisions and the Cross (Ch. 1-4)

The church was divided over leaders—Paul, Apollos, Cephas. Paul reminds them that Christ is not divided and that the cross is the true measure of wisdom.

Lesson: Unity in Christ is greater than loyalty to human leaders.

2. Discipline and Purity (Ch. 5-6)

Paul confronts immorality tolerated in the church and rebukes believers for suing one another in secular courts. He reminds them: "You are not your own; you were bought at a price. Therefore honor God with your bodies." (6:19-20).

Lesson: Holiness matters; the church must reflect God's purity.

3. Marriage and Singleness (Ch. 7)

Paul gives balanced counsel on marriage, celibacy, and divorce, urging believers to honor God in whatever situation they find themselves.

Lesson: Christ must be Lord over our relationships.

4. Liberty and Responsibility (Ch. 8-10)

Paul addresses food offered to idols. Though Christians are free, they must not use freedom to harm others. "So whether you eat or drink or whatever you do, do it all for the glory of God." (10:31).

Lesson: Christian liberty must be guided by love and God's glory.

5. Worship, Gifts, and Love (Ch. 11–14)

Paul corrects abuses in the Lord's Supper and in the use of spiritual gifts. He shows that all gifts are given for the common good. In chapter 13, he presents love as the greatest gift: without love, all gifts are empty.

Lesson: Worship must honor Christ, and love must guide all ministry.

6. The Resurrection (Ch. 15)

Some denied bodily resurrection. Paul declares that Christ has indeed been raised, the firstfruits of those who sleep. Because He lives, we too shall live.

Lesson: The resurrection is the cornerstone of Christian hope.

Christ Revealed in 1 Corinthians

- The Wisdom of God (1:24).
- The Foundation of the Church (3:11).
- The Passover Lamb sacrificed for us (5:7).
- The Rock in the wilderness (10:4).
- The Lord of the Supper (11:23–26).
- The Firstfruits of Resurrection (15:20).

Memory Verse

1 Corinthians 2:2 – "For I resolved to know nothing while I was with you except Jesus Christ and him crucified."

Reflection Questions

1. What were the main causes of division in Corinth, and how do they appear in churches today?

2. Why is the cross central to Paul's message in this letter?
3. How should Christians balance liberty with responsibility?
4. What does 1 Corinthians 13 teach about the supremacy of love?
5. How does chapter 15 strengthen your hope in Christ's resurrection?

Final Exhortation

Students, 1 Corinthians shows us that giftedness without holiness, freedom without love, and worship without order all fall short of God's design. The church must be built not on personalities or human wisdom but on Christ alone.

Let the cross shape your values, love guide your actions, and the resurrection fuel your hope. For the church is not a social club or a debating hall—it is the body of Christ, called to live in unity, holiness, and love until He returns.

~ Eight ~

2 CORINTHIANS

The book of 2 Corinthians is one of Paul's most personal letters. While 1 Corinthians dealt with discipline and correction, 2 Corinthians reveals the heart of a pastor who has been misunderstood, criticized, and wounded, yet continues to love and serve.

Here we see Paul defending his apostleship, describing the hardships of ministry, and reminding the church that the power of Christ shines most brightly through human weakness. This letter shows us that true ministry is not about prestige or outward strength, but about authenticity, humility, and reliance on God's grace.

The central message can be summed up in Paul's testimony: "My grace is sufficient for you, for my power is made perfect in weakness." (2 Corinthians 12:9).

Background of 2 Corinthians

- Author: Paul the Apostle.
- Date: ~AD 55–56, written from Macedonia.
- Audience: The church in Corinth, struggling with false teachers and doubts about Paul's authority.
- Purpose: To defend Paul's apostleship, encourage generosity, and teach that God's power is displayed in weakness.
- Key Verse: "My grace is sufficient for you, for my power is made perfect in weakness." (2 Corinthians 12:9).

Structure of 2 Corinthians

1. Paul's Defense and Comfort (Ch. 1–7)
    - God comforts the afflicted.
    - Paul's sincerity and ministry of reconciliation.
2. The Collection for the Saints (Ch. 8–9)
    - Encouragement to give generously.
3. Paul's Defense Against Critics (Ch. 10–13)
    - False apostles.
    - Paul's sufferings and vision of Christ.

Key Themes of 2 Corinthians

1. God's Comfort in Affliction – He sustains us in suffering.
2. Authentic Ministry – Character over charisma.
3. The Ministry of Reconciliation – Believers are Christ's ambassadors.
4. Generosity in Giving – Grace motivates cheerful giving.
5. Strength in Weakness – God's power is perfected through human weakness.

Exposition and Lessons

1. God's Comfort (Ch. 1)

Paul begins by blessing the "God of all comfort" who comforts us in all our troubles so that we can comfort others.

Lesson: Suffering equips us to minister compassion to others.

2. The New Covenant Ministry (Ch. 3–5)

Paul contrasts the old covenant, written on stone, with the new covenant, written on hearts by the Spirit. He proclaims that believers are new creations in Christ (5:17) and entrusted with the ministry of reconciliation (5:18–20).

Lesson: Every Christian is called to represent Christ as His ambassador.

3. The Call to Holiness and Restoration (Ch. 6–7)

Paul appeals to the Corinthians to separate from ungodliness and be reconciled to him as their spiritual father.

Lesson: True relationships in the body of Christ require holiness and forgiveness.

4. The Grace of Giving (Ch. 8–9)

Paul encourages generous giving to support struggling believers in Jerusalem. He holds up the Macedonians as an example of joyful generosity despite poverty. He reminds them: "God loves a cheerful giver." (9:7).

Lesson: Giving is not a burden but a grace-filled response to God's generosity.

5. Paul's Defense and Boasting in Weakness (Ch. 10–12)

False teachers attacked Paul as unimpressive and weak. Paul responds by boasting not in his strengths but in his weaknesses, recounting his sufferings, beatings, and hardships. He shares his vision of paradise but emphasizes the thorn in his flesh, through which Christ declared: "My grace is sufficient for you."

Lesson: True spiritual authority comes from dependence on God, not human strength.

6. Final Warnings and Encouragement (Ch. 13)

Paul urges the Corinthians to examine themselves to see if they are in the faith and closes with a blessing of grace, love, and fellowship.

Lesson: Self-examination and unity in Christ are essential for a healthy church.

Christ Revealed in 2 Corinthians

- The Comforter in affliction (1:3–5).
- The Image of God (4:4).
- The Reconciler who makes us new (5:17–19).
- The One who was made sin for us (5:21).
- The Lord whose grace is sufficient (12:9).

Memory Verse

2 Corinthians 12:9 – "My grace is sufficient for you, for my power is made perfect in weakness."

Reflection Questions

1. How does Paul describe God's comfort in the midst of suffering?
2. What does it mean to be a "new creation" in Christ?
3. How does the ministry of reconciliation apply to every believer?
4. Why is generosity an expression of God's grace?
5. How does Paul's thorn in the flesh shape our understanding of weakness and grace?

Final Exhortation

Students, 2 Corinthians reveals that authentic Christianity is not about polished appearances or worldly success. It is about being transformed by Christ, living as His ambassadors, and relying on His strength in our weakness.

When you feel inadequate, remember Paul's words: "When I am weak, then I am strong." God's power is not hindered by your weakness—it is displayed through it.

So embrace the grace of Christ, live with integrity, comfort others in their suffering, and serve faithfully as His ambassador. For in our weakness, His glory shines brightest.

~ Nine ~

GALATIANS

The letter to the Galatians is Paul's fiery defense of the gospel of grace. False teachers had infiltrated the churches of Galatia, insisting that Gentile believers must keep the Jewish law—especially circumcision—in order to be saved. Paul responds with urgency: salvation is by grace alone through faith alone in Christ alone.

Galatians has been called the "Magna Carta of Christian Liberty." It boldly proclaims that we are justified by faith, not by works of the law, and that in Christ we are truly free. But this freedom is not a license to sin—it is the power to live by the Spirit and serve one another in love.

The central truth is captured in Paul's words: "It is for freedom that Christ has set us free." (Galatians 5:1).

Background of Galatians

- Author: Paul the Apostle.
- Date: ~AD 48–50, possibly Paul's earliest letter.
- Audience: Churches in the region of Galatia (modern-day Turkey).
- Purpose: To refute legalism, defend justification by faith, and call believers to live in the Spirit.
- Key Verse: "It is for freedom that Christ has set us free." (Galatians 5:1).

Structure of Galatians

1. Defense of Paul's Apostleship (Ch. 1–2)
     ◦ The gospel is revealed by God, not man.
2. Defense of the Gospel of Grace (Ch. 3–4)
     ◦ Abraham's faith as the model.
     ◦ The law as a guardian until Christ.
3. Application of Christian Liberty (Ch. 5–6)
     ◦ Freedom in Christ.
     ◦ Life in the Spirit vs. flesh.
     ◦ Bearing one another's burdens.

Key Themes of Galatians

1. Justification by Faith Alone – Salvation is not by works of the law.
2. Freedom in Christ – Believers are set free from the law's curse.
3. The Spirit-Filled Life – True freedom is walking in the Spirit.
4. Unity in the Gospel – No Jew, Gentile, slave, or free—only one in Christ.
5. The Cross of Christ – Our boast and source of new creation.

Exposition and Lessons

1. No Other Gospel (Ch. 1)

Paul warns that any gospel different from the one he preached is no gospel at all. Even if an angel preaches otherwise, it must be rejected.

Lesson: The gospel of grace must never be compromised.

2. Paul's Defense of His Ministry (Ch. 1-2)

Paul recounts his conversion and confrontation with Peter in Antioch, showing that even apostles must remain true to the gospel.

Lesson: The truth of the gospel stands above personalities or traditions.

3. Justification by Faith (Ch. 3-4)

Paul argues from Abraham's example: he was counted righteous by faith before the law was given. The law was a guardian until Christ, but now we are children of God by faith.

Lesson: Righteousness comes through faith, not rule-keeping.

4. Freedom in Christ (Ch. 5)

Paul declares: "It is for freedom that Christ has set us free." But this freedom must not indulge the flesh. Instead, believers are to walk by the Spirit, bearing the fruit of love, joy, peace, patience, kindness, goodness, faithfulness, gentleness, and self-control.

Lesson: True freedom is not doing whatever we want—it is the Spirit empowering us to live holy lives.

5. Life in the Spirit (Ch. 6)

Paul urges believers to restore the fallen gently, bear one another's burdens, and not grow weary in doing good. He closes with a final boast: "May I never boast except in the cross of our Lord Jesus Christ." (6:14).

Lesson: The Christian life is lived under the cross and in the Spirit, not in legalism or self-reliance.

Christ Revealed in Galatians

- The One who gave Himself for our sins (1:4).
- The Justifier by faith (2:16).
- The Redeemer from the law's curse (3:13).
- The Seed of Abraham (3:16).
- The One formed in us through the Spirit (4:19).
- The Source of new creation (6:15).

Memory Verse

Galatians 5:1 – "It is for freedom that Christ has set us free."

Reflection Questions

1. Why was Paul so urgent about defending the gospel of grace?
2. How does Abraham's example prove justification by faith?
3. What does it mean to be free in Christ?
4. How does walking in the Spirit differ from indulging the flesh?
5. Why is the cross the only boast for the believer?

Final Exhortation

Students, Galatians calls us to stand firm in the freedom Christ has won for us. Legalism enslaves; sin enslaves. But Christ sets us free to live by the Spirit and bear His fruit.

Do not let anything add to or take away from the gospel of grace. Cling to the cross, walk in the Spirit, and serve in love. For in Christ, you are no longer slaves—you are sons and daughters, heirs of the promise, and new creations.

~ Ten ~

EPHESIANS

The letter to the Ephesians is often called the "Crown of Paul's Epistles." It lifts us to the heights of God's eternal plan and shows us the glory of the church as the body of Christ. Unlike Galatians, which defends freedom from the law, or Corinthians, which corrects problems, Ephesians is a sweeping vision of who we are in Christ and how we are to live in Him.

Paul reminds us that before the foundation of the world, God chose us in Christ. Through His blood we have redemption, forgiveness, and an inheritance sealed by the Holy Spirit. Then Paul calls us to live worthy of this calling—walking in unity, purity, love, light, wisdom, and strength.

The central theme can be summed up: "Blessed be the God and Father of our Lord Jesus Christ, who has blessed us in Christ with every spiritual blessing in the heavenly places." (Ephesians 1:3).

Background of Ephesians

- Author: Paul the Apostle.
- Date: ~AD 60–62, written from prison in Rome.
- Audience: Believers in Ephesus (and likely surrounding churches in Asia Minor).
- Purpose: To exalt Christ, reveal the church's identity, and instruct believers to live out their calling.

- Key Verse: "For it is by grace you have been saved, through faith—and this is not from yourselves, it is the gift of God—not by works, so that no one can boast." (Ephesians 2:8–9).

Structure of Ephesians

1. Our Position in Christ (Ch. 1–3)
   ◦ Chosen, redeemed, and sealed.
   ◦ Jew and Gentile united in one body.
   ◦ Paul's prayer for strength and fullness.
2. Our Practice in Christ (Ch. 4–6)
   ◦ Unity and maturity in the body.
   ◦ Walking in holiness and love.
   ◦ Spirit-filled relationships.
   ◦ The armor of God for spiritual warfare.

Key Themes of Ephesians

1. Spiritual Blessings in Christ – Every believer is richly blessed.
2. The Mystery of the Church – Jew and Gentile united as one body.
3. Salvation by Grace – A gift, not earned by works.
4. Unity and Maturity – Growing together in love.
5. Spiritual Warfare – Standing firm in God's armor.

Exposition and Lessons

1. Chosen and Blessed (Ch. 1)

Paul begins with a soaring doxology, praising God for choosing us, redeeming us through Christ's blood, and sealing us with the Spirit.

Lesson: Our identity is rooted in God's eternal plan, not our performance.

2. Saved by Grace (Ch. 2)

Paul describes humanity as "dead in transgressions," but God made us alive with Christ. Salvation is God's gift, not our works. We are His workmanship, created for good works.

Lesson: Grace is the foundation of salvation and the motivation for service.

3. Unity in Christ (Ch. 2-3)

Christ broke down the wall between Jew and Gentile, creating one new humanity. The church is God's dwelling place, revealing His wisdom to the world.

Lesson: Unity in the church is not optional—it is essential to God's plan.

4. Walking Worthy (Ch. 4-5)

Paul urges believers to walk in humility, gentleness, patience, and love. He contrasts the old life of darkness with the new life of light. Marriage is presented as a picture of Christ and the church.

Lesson: Our calling demands a transformed lifestyle marked by love and holiness.

5. The Armor of God (Ch. 6)

Paul concludes with a call to stand firm against the devil's schemes. Believers must put on the full armor of God: truth, righteousness, readiness, faith, salvation, the Word, and prayer.

Lesson: Spiritual warfare is real, but victory is assured in Christ.

Christ Revealed in Ephesians

- The Head of the church (1:22–23).
- The One who gives redemption through His blood (1:7).
- The Cornerstone of God's household (2:20).
- The One who dwells in our hearts through faith (3:17).
- The Giver of gifts to the church (4:7–11).
- The Bridegroom who loves the church (5:25).
- The Warrior King who equips us with armor (6:10–17).

Memory Verse

Ephesians 2:8–9 – "For it is by grace you have been saved, through faith—and this is not from yourselves, it is the gift of God—not by works, so that no one can boast."

Reflection Questions

1. What does it mean that believers are "blessed with every spiritual blessing in Christ"?
2. How does Ephesians describe salvation by grace?
3. Why is unity in the church central to God's plan?
4. How do Spirit-filled relationships reflect Christ and the church?
5. What does it look like to put on the full armor of God in daily life?

Final Exhortation

Students, Ephesians lifts our eyes from earthly struggles to heavenly realities. It shows us who we are in Christ—chosen, redeemed, sealed, and seated with Him. And it calls us to live out this identity with love, unity, and strength.

Never forget: you are God's workmanship, created for good works. You are part of a glorious body, the church, destined to display His wisdom. And you are equipped for victory in Christ's armor.

So walk worthy of your calling, rooted in grace, united in love, and standing strong in the Lord.

~ Eleven ~

PHILIPPIANS

The letter to the Philippians is Paul's joy-filled message from prison. Unlike Galatians, which defends grace, or Corinthians, which corrects problems, Philippians is deeply personal. It is a thank-you letter to the believers in Philippi for their partnership in the gospel, but it is also a pastoral exhortation to stand firm, rejoice always, and press toward Christ.

Even while chained in a Roman cell, Paul overflows with joy. Why? Because his joy is not rooted in circumstances but in Christ. He reminds us that joy flows from knowing Jesus, serving others, and pressing on toward the prize of heaven.

The theme verse is: "Rejoice in the Lord always. I will say it again: Rejoice!" (Philippians 4:4).

Background of Philippians

- Author: Paul the Apostle.
- Date: ~AD 61, written during Paul's imprisonment in Rome.
- Audience: The church at Philippi, the first church planted in Europe.
- Purpose: To thank them for support, encourage unity and humility, and call them to joy in Christ.
- Key Verse: "For to me, to live is Christ and to die is gain." (Philippians 1:21).

Structure of Philippians

1. Partnership in the Gospel (Ch. 1)
     ◦ Thanksgiving and prayer.
     ◦ Paul's chains advance the gospel.
     ◦ Christ magnified in life and death.
2. The Example of Christ (Ch. 2)
     ◦ Humility and servanthood.
     ◦ The Christ hymn (2:5–11).
     ◦ Examples: Timothy and Epaphroditus.
3. Pressing Toward the Goal (Ch. 3)
     ◦ Warning against legalism.
     ◦ Paul's pursuit of Christ.
4. Joy and Peace in the Lord (Ch. 4)
     ◦ Rejoice always.
     ◦ Peace that passes understanding.
     ◦ Contentment in all circumstances.

Key Themes of Philippians

1. Joy in Christ – Rooted not in circumstances but in the Lord.
2. Unity in the Church – Standing firm together in love.
3. Humility and Service – Modeled after Christ's self-emptying.
4. Pressing Toward the Prize – Pursuing Christ above all else.
5. Contentment and Peace – Found in Christ's strength.

Exposition and Lessons

1. Joy in Chains (Ch. 1)

Paul rejoices that his imprisonment has advanced the gospel. Even if others preach Christ out of envy, he still rejoices because Christ is proclaimed. His confidence is captured in 1:21: "For to me, to live is Christ and to die is gain."

Lesson: Joy is not based on freedom or comfort but on Christ.

2. The Example of Christ (Ch. 2)

Paul exhorts the church to unity and humility: "In your relationships with one another, have the same mindset as Christ Jesus." He then quotes the great Christ hymn: Jesus humbled Himself, took on the form of a servant, and became obedient to death on a cross—therefore God exalted Him above every name.

Lesson: True greatness is found in humility and service.

3. Pressing Toward the Goal (Ch. 3)

Paul warns against placing confidence in the flesh. Though he had every reason to boast as a Jew, he counts it all loss compared to knowing Christ. He presses on toward the goal for the prize of God's heavenly calling.

Lesson: Knowing Christ is greater than any earthly achievement.

4. Joy, Peace, and Contentment (Ch. 4)

Paul encourages believers to rejoice always, pray with thanksgiving, and rest in God's peace. He testifies that he has learned the secret of contentment in every circumstance: "I can do all this through him who gives me strength." (4:13).

Lesson: Peace and contentment come not from possessions but from Christ's presence.

Christ Revealed in Philippians

- The Exalted Lord (2:9–11).
- The Servant who humbled Himself to death (2:5–8).

• The Prize worth pursuing (3:8, 14).
• The Source of peace and strength (4:7, 13).

Memory Verse

Philippians 4:4 – "Rejoice in the Lord always. I will say it again: Rejoice!"

Reflection Questions

1. Why was Paul able to rejoice even in prison?
2. How does the Christ hymn in Philippians 2 model humility and service?
3. What does Paul mean by "to live is Christ and to die is gain"?
4. How can we learn to be content in all circumstances?
5. How does pressing toward the goal challenge your own priorities?

Final Exhortation

Students, Philippians teaches us that true joy does not come from circumstances but from Christ. Joy is found in serving others, humbling ourselves like Jesus, and pressing forward to know Him more.

If you are in hardship, rejoice. If you are in conflict, choose humility. If you are weary, press on. And if you are anxious, pray and rest in God's peace.

Remember: to live is Christ, and to die is gain. That is the secret of joy, the strength of peace, and the hope of glory.

~ Twelve ~

COLOSSIANS

The book of Colossians exalts Jesus Christ as supreme over all creation and sufficient for all our spiritual needs. The church in Colossae was threatened by false teachers who mixed Jewish legalism, Greek philosophy, and mystical practices. They claimed believers needed "something more" than Christ—more rituals, more visions, more human wisdom.

Paul writes with passion to declare that Christ is all we need. He is the image of the invisible God, the Creator and Sustainer of all things, the Head of the church, and the fullness of God dwelling in human flesh. In Him, we are complete.

The message of Colossians is summed up in Paul's declaration: "He is before all things, and in him all things hold together." (Colossians 1:17).

Background of Colossians

- Author: Paul the Apostle.
- Date: ~AD 60–62, written from prison in Rome.
- Audience: Believers in Colossae, a small city in Asia Minor.
- Purpose: To combat false teachings and affirm Christ's supremacy and sufficiency.
- Key Verse: "The Son is the image of the invisible God, the firstborn over all creation." (Colossians 1:15).

Structure of Colossians

1. The Supremacy of Christ (Ch. 1)
   - Thanksgiving and prayer.
   - The Christ hymn (1:15–20).
2. The Sufficiency of Christ (Ch. 2)
   - Warning against false philosophies and legalism.
3. The New Life in Christ (Ch. 3–4)
   - Putting off the old self, putting on the new.
   - Instructions for relationships.
   - Final greetings and encouragements.

Key Themes of Colossians

1. The Supremacy of Christ – He is Lord over creation and the church.
2. The Sufficiency of Christ – In Him, believers are complete.
3. False Teachings Refuted – Legalism, mysticism, and human traditions.
4. Union with Christ – Believers are buried and raised with Him.
5. New Life in Christ – Practical holiness in daily living.

Exposition and Lessons

1. Christ Supreme (Ch. 1)

Paul opens with prayer for the Colossians, then exalts Christ in one of the most profound passages in Scripture: He is the image of God, Creator of all, Sustainer of life, Head of the church, and Reconciler through His blood.

Lesson: Christ is not just part of life—He is the center and sustainer of life.

2. Complete in Christ (Ch. 2)

Paul warns against deceptive philosophies, legalism, and mystical experiences that detract from Christ. He reminds them that they are complete in Him, having been buried with Him in baptism and raised with Him through faith.

Lesson: Nothing needs to be added to Christ—He is sufficient for salvation and growth.

3. Living the New Life (Ch. 3)

Believers are called to set their hearts on things above, put to death earthly sins, and put on compassion, kindness, humility, gentleness, and patience. Love binds everything together in perfect unity.

Lesson: New life in Christ is not theory—it transforms daily behavior.

4. Christ in Relationships (Ch. 3–4)

Paul gives instructions for households: wives, husbands, children, parents, servants, and masters. Every role is to be lived "as unto the Lord."

Lesson: Christ transforms not only personal character but also family and work life.

5. Perseverance in Prayer and Mission (Ch. 4)

Paul urges prayer, watchfulness, and wisdom in witness. He highlights co-workers in the gospel, reminding us that ministry is teamwork under Christ's headship.

Lesson: Prayer and mission are central to a Christ-centered life.

Christ Revealed in Colossians

- The Image of the Invisible God (1:15).
- The Creator and Sustainer of all things (1:16–17).
- The Head of the Church (1:18).
- The Fullness of God in bodily form (2:9).
- The Victor over powers and authorities (2:15).
- The Source of new life (3:1–4).

Memory Verse

Colossians 1:17 – "He is before all things, and in him all things hold together."

Reflection Questions

1. Why is it important that Christ is described as the image of the invisible God?
2. How does Paul refute the idea that we need "something more" than Christ?
3. What does it mean to be complete in Christ?
4. How does Colossians 3 challenge your daily lifestyle?
5. In what ways does Christ's supremacy give you confidence in uncertain times?

Final Exhortation

Students, Colossians reminds us that Christ is supreme above all things and sufficient for every need. Do not be deceived by philosophies, traditions, or spiritual fads that promise more. You already have everything in Christ.

Live with confidence, knowing that the fullness of God dwells in Him and that you are complete in Him. Set your heart on things above, let Christ rule in your relationships, and persevere in prayer and witness.

For in Christ, all things hold together—and in Him, your life is secure.

~ Thirteen ~

1 THESSALONIANS

The book of 1 Thessalonians is one of Paul's earliest letters, written to a young church facing persecution. Despite their trials, the Thessalonians became a model of faith, hope, and love. Paul writes to encourage them, correct misunderstandings about Christ's return, and call them to holy living.

This letter shines with pastoral warmth. Paul reassures these new believers that their suffering is not in vain, that their loved ones who died in Christ will rise again, and that they themselves should live in readiness for the coming of the Lord.

The heart of 1 Thessalonians is found in "For the Lord himself will come down from heaven, with a loud command, with the voice of the archangel and with the trumpet call of God, and the dead in Christ will rise first." (1 Thessalonians 4:16).

Background of 1 Thessalonians

- Author: Paul the Apostle (with Silas and Timothy).
- Date: ~AD 50–51, from Corinth.
- Audience: The church in Thessalonica, a key city in Macedonia.
- Purpose: To encourage perseverance, clarify teaching on the Lord's return, and call believers to holiness.

- Key Verse: "For the Lord himself will come down from heaven... and the dead in Christ will rise first." (1 Thessalonians 4:16).

Structure of 1 Thessalonians

1. Thanksgiving for the Church (Ch. 1)
    - Faith, love, and hope in action.
2. Paul's Ministry and Affection (Ch. 2–3)
    - Paul's example and encouragement in persecution.
3. Instructions for Holy Living (Ch. 4)
    - Sanctification, sexual purity, brotherly love.
4. Hope in Christ's Return (Ch. 4–5)
    - The rapture of believers.
    - The Day of the Lord.
    - Exhortations for watchfulness and readiness.

Key Themes of 1 Thessalonians

1. Faith, Love, and Hope – The marks of a healthy church.
2. Perseverance in Persecution – Encouragement for trials.
3. Holiness in Daily Life – God's will is sanctification.
4. The Coming of the Lord – Comfort for grieving believers.
5. Readiness and Watchfulness – Living in light of eternity.

Exposition and Lessons

1. Faith, Love, and Hope (Ch. 1)

Paul thanks God for the Thessalonians' "work of faith, labor of love, and steadfastness of hope." Their testimony spread throughout the region.

Lesson: A church grounded in faith, love, and hope impacts the world.

2. Paul's Ministry Example (Ch. 2-3)

Paul reminds them how he ministered with gentleness, like a nursing mother, and with exhortation, like a father. He rejoices that they received the word as God's truth, not man's opinion.

Lesson: Ministry is relational, marked by love, sacrifice, and authenticity.

3. Call to Holiness (Ch. 4:1-12)

Paul urges them to live to please God, abstain from sexual immorality, and love one another more and more.

Lesson: Holiness is God's will for every believer.

4. The Return of Christ (Ch. 4:13-18)

Paul comforts the grieving by explaining that when Christ returns, the dead in Christ will rise first, and then living believers will be caught up together with them to meet the Lord.

Lesson: Our hope is not in avoiding death but in resurrection and reunion with Christ.

5. The Day of the Lord (Ch. 5:1-11)

Paul warns that the Day of the Lord will come like a thief in the night. Believers must be alert and sober, clothed with faith, love, and hope.

Lesson: We must live ready for Christ's return, not in fear but in faith.

6. *Final Exhortations (Ch. 5:12–28)*

Paul gives practical instructions: respect leaders, encourage the fainthearted, rejoice always, pray continually, give thanks in all circumstances, and avoid evil.

Lesson: Christian maturity is expressed in daily obedience and gratitude.

Christ Revealed in 1 Thessalonians

- The One who delivers us from wrath (1:10).
- The Coming Lord (3:13; 4:16).
- The Resurrection and Life (4:14–16).
- The Prince of Peace (5:23).

Memory Verse

1 Thessalonians 4:16 – "For the Lord himself will come down from heaven, with a loud command, with the voice of the archangel and with the trumpet call of God, and the dead in Christ will rise first."

Reflection Questions

1. How did the Thessalonians model faith, love, and hope?
2. Why was Paul's ministry style important for building trust in the young church?
3. What does it mean that sanctification is God's will for every believer?
4. How does Paul comfort those grieving the loss of loved ones in Christ?
5. What does living in readiness for Christ's return look like for you?

Final Exhortation

Students, 1 Thessalonians teaches us to endure hardship with hope, live holy lives, and eagerly await Christ's return. This world is not our home; we are citizens of heaven awaiting our King.

So do not lose heart in trials. Do not compromise in holiness. And do not grow weary in watching and waiting. For the trumpet will sound, the dead in Christ will rise, and together we will meet the Lord in the air.

And Paul assures us: "And so we will be with the Lord forever. Therefore encourage one another with these words." (4:17–18).

~ Fourteen ~

2 THESSALONIANS

The book of 2 Thessalonians was written to a young church still facing persecution, but also dealing with confusion about the Day of the Lord. Some believers feared they had missed Christ's return. Others, convinced His coming was imminent, stopped working and became idle.

Paul writes to comfort the persecuted, clarify the truth about Christ's return, and correct disorderly behavior. He reassures them that the Day of the Lord has not yet come, describes events that must precede it, and urges them to stand firm in the gospel.

The central message is found in "So then, brothers and sisters, stand firm and hold fast to the teachings we passed on to you." (2 Thessalonians 2:15).

Background of 2 Thessalonians

- Author: Paul the Apostle (with Silas and Timothy).
- Date: ~AD 51–52, shortly after 1 Thessalonians.
- Audience: The church in Thessalonica.
- Purpose: To encourage perseverance, correct false teaching about the Day of the Lord, and exhort believers to responsible living.
- Key Verse: "So then, brothers and sisters, stand firm and hold fast to the teachings we passed on to you." (2 Thessalonians 2:15).

Structure of 2 Thessalonians

1. Encouragement in Persecution (Ch. 1)
   - God's justice will prevail.
   - The persecuted will find rest when Christ returns.
2. Clarification of the Day of the Lord (Ch. 2)
   - False claims corrected.
   - The rebellion and "man of lawlessness" revealed.
   - Standing firm in the truth.
3. Exhortations for Responsible Living (Ch. 3)
   - Warning against idleness.
   - Call to discipline and obedience.

Key Themes of 2 Thessalonians

1. Perseverance in Persecution – God's justice will vindicate His people.
2. The Day of the Lord – Events must precede Christ's return.
3. The Man of Lawlessness – A figure of rebellion before the end.
4. Standing Firm in Truth – Holding fast to apostolic teaching.
5. Responsible Living – Working diligently while waiting for Christ.

Exposition and Lessons

1. Comfort for the Persecuted (Ch. 1)

Paul begins by commending their growing faith and endurance. He assures them that God will repay affliction to their oppressors and give rest to His people when Jesus is revealed in glory.

Lesson: Persecution is temporary; Christ's justice is eternal.

2. Clarifying the Day of the Lord (Ch. 2:1–12)

Some claimed the Day of the Lord had already come. Paul counters this by teaching that two events must occur first: the great rebellion and the revealing of the "man of lawlessness," who exalts himself above God. This figure will be destroyed by the breath of Christ's mouth at His coming.

Lesson: Do not be shaken by false teaching—God's plan unfolds in His time.

3. Stand Firm in the Truth (Ch. 2:13–17)

Paul reminds them they were chosen for salvation through belief in the truth. He calls them to hold firmly to the teachings he delivered.

Lesson: Stability in faith comes from clinging to God's Word.

4. Warning Against Idleness (Ch. 3:6–15)

Some believers had stopped working, expecting Christ's return at any moment. Paul rebukes this, setting himself as an example of hard work. He declares, "The one who is unwilling to work shall not eat." (3:10).

Lesson: Waiting for Christ is active, not passive—believers must work faithfully.

5. Final Blessing (Ch. 3:16–18)

Paul prays that the Lord of peace Himself will give them peace at all times in every way.

Lesson: Christ alone is the source of lasting peace in the midst of trials.

Christ Revealed in 2 Thessalonians

- The Righteous Judge (1:5–7).
- The Glorious Lord returning with angels (1:7–10).
- The Destroyer of the man of lawlessness (2:8).
- The Giver of eternal comfort and good hope (2:16).
- The Lord of peace (3:16).

Memory Verse

2 Thessalonians 2:15 – "So then, brothers and sisters, stand firm and hold fast to the teachings we passed on to you."

Reflection Questions

1. How does Paul comfort persecuted believers in chapter 1?
2. What must occur before the Day of the Lord, according to Paul?
3. Who is the "man of lawlessness," and what is his fate?
4. Why is it important to stand firm in apostolic teaching?
5. How does Paul address idleness, and what lessons does this hold for us today?

Final Exhortation

Students, 2 Thessalonians reminds us that persecution is not the end of the story, and confusion about Christ's return must not shake our faith. We are called to stand firm, hold fast, and live faithfully while we wait for Him.

Do not let fear, false teaching, or idleness distract you. Christ will return in glory, justice will prevail, and His people will share in His rest. Until then, work diligently, live responsibly, and anchor yourself in His Word.

~ Fifteen ~

1 TIMOTHY

The book of 1 Timothy is one of Paul's Pastoral Epistles, written to his spiritual son Timothy, whom he had left in Ephesus to shepherd the church. Unlike Romans or Galatians, which address doctrinal issues, this letter gives practical instruction for church leadership, sound teaching, and godly living.

Paul reminds Timothy that the church is "the household of God, the church of the living God, the pillar and foundation of the truth" (3:15). Because of this, leaders must be above reproach, false teachers must be opposed, and believers must pursue godliness.

The central truth can be summarized in Paul's exhortation: "Fight the good fight of the faith. Take hold of the eternal life to which you were called." (1 Timothy 6:12).

Background of 1 Timothy

- Author: Paul the Apostle.
- Date: ~AD 63–65, after Paul's first Roman imprisonment.
- Audience: Timothy in Ephesus, overseeing the church.
- Purpose: To instruct Timothy on church leadership, sound doctrine, and personal godliness.
- Key Verse: "Fight the good fight of the faith." (1 Timothy 6:12).

Structure of 1 Timothy

1. Confronting False Teachers (Ch. 1)
   - Warning against myths and speculation.
   - The law used lawfully.
   - Paul's testimony of grace.
2. Worship and Church Order (Ch. 2–3)
   - Prayer for all people.
   - Roles of men and women in worship.
   - Qualifications for overseers and deacons.
3. Instructions for Godly Living (Ch. 4–6)
   - Guarding against false asceticism.
   - Example in speech, conduct, love, faith, purity.
   - Care for widows and elders.
   - Warning against greed and love of money.
   - Call to pursue righteousness and fight the good fight.

Key Themes of 1 Timothy

1. Sound Doctrine – Teaching must be rooted in truth.
2. Church Leadership – Elders and deacons must meet godly qualifications.
3. Prayer and Worship – Central to church life.
4. Godliness and Contentment – Greater than worldly wealth.
5. Faithful Ministry – A spiritual fight requiring perseverance.

Exposition and Lessons

1. Guarding the Gospel (Ch. 1)

Paul charges Timothy to silence false teachers who misuse the law and promote controversies. He shares his own story of mercy, reminding Timothy of the transforming power of grace.

Lesson: Ministry begins with guarding the gospel from distortion.

2. Worship and Prayer (Ch. 2)

Paul urges prayer for all people, especially leaders, that the church may live in peace. He emphasizes orderly worship and the proper roles within the gathered body.

Lesson: Prayer is not optional—it is the lifeline of the church.

3. Leadership in God's House (Ch. 3)

Paul lays out qualifications for overseers and deacons. Leaders must be above reproach, self-controlled, hospitable, able to teach, not greedy, and faithful in family life.

Lesson: Character, not charisma, qualifies a person for leadership.

4. Example of Godliness (Ch. 4)

Paul warns against false asceticism and urges Timothy: "Don't let anyone look down on you because you are young, but set an example for the believers." (4:12).

Lesson: Ministry requires modeling godliness, not just teaching it.

5. Instructions for the Household (Ch. 5)

Paul gives practical instructions for widows, elders, and relationships in the church. Care and respect must govern family and church life alike.

Lesson: God's church must be a place of honor, care, and accountability.

6. *The Good Fight of Faith (Ch. 6)*

Paul warns against greed, declaring: "The love of money is a root of all kinds of evil." He urges Timothy to flee evil, pursue righteousness, and fight the good fight of the faith.

Lesson: Faithful ministry demands endurance, courage, and eternal perspective.

Christ Revealed in 1 Timothy

- The Savior of sinners (1:15).
- The One Mediator between God and humanity (2:5).
- The Mystery of Godliness made manifest (3:16).
- The Lord who gives life and appearing in glory (6:14–16).

Memory Verse

1 Timothy 6:12 – "Fight the good fight of the faith. Take hold of the eternal life to which you were called."

Reflection Questions

1. Why is it important for church leaders to meet the qualifications in chapter 3?
2. How does Paul describe sound doctrine in contrast to false teaching?
3. What does it mean to "set an example" in speech, conduct, love, faith, and purity?
4. Why is contentment with godliness greater than worldly wealth?
5. How can believers today "fight the good fight of the faith"?

Final Exhortation

Students, 1 Timothy reminds us that the church is the household of God, entrusted with the gospel. It is not a place for personal ambition or worldly gain, but for truth, holiness, and service.

You too are called to guard the gospel, pray faithfully, pursue godliness, and endure hardship with courage. Let your life reflect Christ, your leadership be rooted in integrity, and your ministry be marked by perseverance.

Fight the good fight, beloved, and take hold of eternal life with unwavering faith.

~ Sixteen ~

2 TIMOTHY

The book of 2 Timothy is Paul's last letter, written from a Roman dungeon as he awaited execution. Unlike the victorious tone of Philippians or the doctrinal depth of Romans, this epistle carries the weight of a father's final words to his beloved son in the faith, Timothy.

Paul knows the end is near: "I have fought the good fight, I have finished the race, I have kept the faith." (2 Timothy 4:7). Yet, he writes not in despair but with courage, urging Timothy to endure hardship, guard the gospel, and preach the Word faithfully in the face of opposition.

This letter is a call to faithful endurance in a world that resists truth. It is as relevant to us today as it was to Timothy nearly 2,000 years ago.

Background of 2 Timothy

- Author: Paul the Apostle.
- Date: ~AD 66–67, during Paul's second Roman imprisonment.
- Audience: Timothy in Ephesus, facing false teachers and persecution.
- Purpose: To encourage Timothy to endure, remain faithful, and continue preaching the Word.

- Key Verse: "Preach the word; be prepared in season and out of season; correct, rebuke and encourage—with great patience and careful instruction." (2 Timothy 4:2).

Structure of 2 Timothy

1. Endurance in the Gospel (Ch. 1)
   - Guard the good deposit entrusted to you.
2. Strength for Ministry (Ch. 2)
   - The soldier, athlete, and farmer illustrations.
   - Endurance in suffering.l
3. Perseverance in the Last Days (Ch. 3)
   - Difficult times ahead.
   - The power of Scripture for teaching and equipping.
4. Faithfulness to the End (Ch. 4)
   - Preach the Word faithfully.
   - Paul's farewell testimony.

Key Themes of 2 Timothy

1. Faithful Endurance – Holding firm in suffering.
2. Guarding the Gospel – Preserving truth against false teachers.
3. The Power of God's Word – Scripture equips for every good work.
4. Mentorship and Legacy – Passing faith to the next generation.
5. Finishing Well – A life poured out for Christ.

Exposition and Lessons

1. Guard the Gospel (Ch. 1)

Paul urges Timothy not to be ashamed of the testimony about Christ but to join in suffering for the gospel. The Spirit gives power, love, and self-discipline.

Lesson: The gospel must be guarded and proclaimed with courage.

2. Endure Hardship (Ch. 2)

Paul uses vivid illustrations: the soldier who endures hardship, the athlete who competes by the rules, and the farmer who works hard for the harvest. Timothy must pass on truth to faithful people who will teach others.

Lesson: Ministry requires endurance, discipline, and multiplication of disciples.

3. Last Days Warnings (Ch. 3)

Paul warns that terrible times will come, with people being lovers of self, money, and pleasure rather than God. He reminds Timothy of the sufficiency of Scripture: "All Scripture is God-breathed and is useful for teaching, rebuking, correcting and training in righteousness." (3:16).

Lesson: In a world of deception, God's Word is the anchor of truth.

4. Preach the Word (Ch. 4)

Paul charges Timothy to preach the Word in every season—when it's convenient and when it's not. He warns of people with itching ears who will turn from truth. Paul then shares his own testimony: he has finished the race and awaits the crown of righteousness.

Lesson: Ministry must be rooted in God's Word and lived with eternity in view.

Christ Revealed in 2 Timothy

- The Savior who abolished death (1:10).
- The Faithful Judge who will reward His servants (4:8).
- The Lord who strengthens His people (4:17).
- The Deliverer who rescues from every evil attack (4:18).

Memory Verse

2 Timothy 4:7 – "I have fought the good fight, I have finished the race, I have kept the faith."

Reflection Questions

1. How does Paul encourage Timothy to endure suffering for the gospel?
2. What do the soldier, athlete, and farmer illustrations teach us about ministry?
3. Why is Scripture essential for equipping believers in the last days?
4. How can we remain faithful when people "turn aside to myths"?
5. What does it mean to finish the race well in your own life?

Final Exhortation

Students, 2 Timothy is a call to endurance, courage, and faithfulness. Paul shows us that ministry is not about comfort or popularity but about guarding the truth, enduring hardship, and passing the baton of faith.

One day, each of us will come to the end of our race. May we, like Paul, be able to say: "I have fought the good fight, I have finished the race, I have kept the faith." Let us live not for earthly applause but for the eternal crown of righteousness the Lord will give.

~ Seventeen ~

TITUS

The letter to Titus is one of Paul's Pastoral Epistles, written to guide his trusted co-worker in establishing strong churches on the island of Crete. This short but powerful book emphasizes two inseparable truths: sound doctrine and good works.

Paul makes it clear that truth and practice go hand in hand. Right teaching produces right living, and the grace of God not only saves us but also trains us to live godly lives.

The message of Titus can be summarized in Paul's words: "For the grace of God has appeared that offers salvation to all people. It teaches us to say 'No' to ungodliness and worldly passions, and to live self-controlled, upright and godly lives in this present age." (Titus 2:11–12).

Background of Titus

- Author: Paul the Apostle.
- Date: ~AD 63–65, after Paul's first Roman imprisonment.
- Audience: Titus, left in Crete to organize and strengthen the churches.
- Purpose: To appoint qualified leaders, teach sound doctrine, and urge believers to live godly lives.
- Key Verse: "For the grace of God has appeared... it teaches us to say 'No' to ungodliness and worldly passions." (Titus 2:11–12).

Structure of Titus

1. Qualified Leaders (Ch. 1)
    - Elders must be above reproach.
    - Rebuke false teachers.
2. Sound Doctrine and Godly Living (Ch. 2)
    - Instructions for older men, older women, young women, young men, and slaves.
    - Grace teaches holiness.
3. Good Works in Society (Ch. 3)
    - Submission to authorities.
    - Salvation by grace, not works.
    - Devotion to good works as evidence of faith.

Key Themes of Titus

1. Sound Doctrine – Truth is essential for healthy churches.
2. Godly Leadership – Elders must lead with integrity and truth.
3. Grace and Godliness – Grace saves and transforms.
4. Good Works – The fruit of salvation and testimony to the world.
5. Hope of Eternal Life – Grounded in God's unchanging promise.

Exposition and Lessons

1. The Call for Qualified Elders (Ch. 1)

Paul instructs Titus to appoint elders who are blameless, faithful in marriage, self-controlled, hospitable, and able to teach sound doctrine. They must silence false teachers who deceive for selfish gain.

Lesson: The health of the church depends on godly, qualified leaders.

2. Sound Doctrine for All (Ch. 2)

Paul gives instructions tailored to different groups in the church—older men and women, younger men and women, and servants. He emphasizes self-control, dignity, and good teaching. The motivation comes from grace: it trains believers to live holy lives.

Lesson: Sound teaching shapes everyday living across every stage of life.

3. Grace that Transforms (Ch. 2:11-15)

Paul highlights that grace is not only the basis of salvation but also the power for sanctification. Grace teaches us to renounce sin and live for God while we wait for the blessed hope—the return of Christ.

Lesson: True grace does not excuse sin; it empowers holiness.

4. Good Works as a Witness (Ch. 3)

Paul urges believers to be submissive to rulers, gentle, and peaceable. He reminds them of their past sinfulness but celebrates salvation by God's mercy, not works. He stresses that those who trust in God must devote themselves to doing what is good.

Lesson: Good works are not the root of salvation but the fruit of salvation.

5. Avoiding Foolish Controversies (Ch. 3:9–15)

Paul warns against divisive arguments and false teachers. Titus is to focus on what builds up the church and glorifies Christ.

Lesson: The church must avoid distractions and stay focused on gospel truth.

Christ Revealed in Titus

- The Savior who brings salvation to all (2:11).
- The Blessed Hope—our coming King (2:13).
- The One who gave Himself to redeem us (2:14).
- The Justifier by His mercy (3:5–7).

Memory Verse

Titus 2:11–12 – "For the grace of God has appeared that offers salvation to all people. It teaches us to say 'No' to ungodliness and worldly passions, and to live self-controlled, upright and godly lives in this present age."

Reflection Questions

1. Why is it important for church leaders to be qualified by character, not just ability?
2. How does grace both save us and teach us to live holy lives?
3. Why are good works essential as evidence of faith?
4. How does Paul balance salvation by grace with the call to obedience?
5. What distractions or controversies must the church avoid today?

Final Exhortation

Students, Titus shows us that healthy churches require both sound doctrine and godly living. Grace is not a free pass to sin but a transforming power that teaches holiness and produces good works.

As future leaders and servants of Christ, remember this: the credibility of the church is tied to the integrity of its leaders and the witness of its people. Preach truth. Live truth. Model truth. And let the grace of God train you to live uprightly while you await Christ's return.

~ Eighteen ~

PHILEMON

The letter to Philemon is the shortest of Paul's writings, yet it carries one of the most powerful lessons in the New Testament: the transforming power of the gospel in relationships.

Philemon, a wealthy believer in Colossae, had a slave named Onesimus who ran away and likely wronged him in some way. In God's providence, Onesimus encountered Paul, came to faith in Christ, and became a faithful helper to the apostle. Paul now writes to Philemon, urging him not to punish Onesimus but to receive him back no longer as a slave but as a beloved brother in Christ.

This letter demonstrates that the gospel does not only reconcile us to God but also reconciles us to one another. It challenges social norms and points to the radical equality found in Christ.

The heart of Philemon is captured in Paul's plea: "Perhaps the reason he was separated from you for a little while was that you might have him back forever—no longer as a slave, but better than a slave, as a dear brother." (Philemon 15–16).

Background of Philemon

- Author: Paul the Apostle.
- Date: ~AD 60–62, written from prison in Rome.
- Audience: Philemon, his household, and the church that met in his home.

- Purpose: To appeal for reconciliation between Philemon and Onesimus.
- Key Verse: "No longer as a slave, but better than a slave, as a dear brother." (Philemon 16).

Structure of Philemon

1. Greeting and Thanksgiving (v. 1–7)
     ◦ Paul's gratitude for Philemon's faith and love.
2. Paul's Appeal for Onesimus (v. 8–16)
     ◦ Onesimus as Paul's "son" in the faith.
     ◦ Appeal to receive him as a brother.
3. Paul's Offer and Confidence (v. 17–22)
     ◦ Paul offers to repay any debt.
     ◦ Confidence in Philemon's obedience.
4. Final Greetings (v. 23–25)

Key Themes of Philemon

1. The Power of the Gospel – It transforms hearts and relationships.
2. Forgiveness and Reconciliation – Believers are called to forgive as Christ forgave.
3. Equality in Christ – Social barriers are broken down in the body of Christ.
4. Intercession in Love – Paul models advocacy and mediation.
5. The Fellowship of Faith – True fellowship produces action.

Exposition and Lessons

1. Thanksgiving for Philemon (v. 1-7)

Paul begins by affirming Philemon's love and faith, setting the stage for his appeal.

Lesson: Affirmation prepares the heart for correction and challenge.

2. An Appeal in Love (v. 8–16)

Rather than command, Paul appeals "on the basis of love." Onesimus is now Paul's "son" in the faith and must be received as more than a slave—as a brother.

Lesson: The gospel transforms social roles into spiritual relationships.

3. Partnership in the Gospel (v. 17–22)

Paul offers to cover any debt Onesimus owes. He reminds Philemon of his own debt to Paul and expresses confidence that Philemon will do even more than asked.

Lesson: True fellowship involves sacrifice, forgiveness, and restoration.

4. Closing Greetings (v. 23–25)

Paul's greetings include other faithful workers, showing that reconciliation is not just personal but a testimony to the wider church.

Lesson: How we handle relationships affects the witness of the entire body of Christ.

Christ Revealed in Philemon

- The Advocate who intercedes for us (v. 10).
- The One who paid our debt (v. 18–19).
- The Brother who restores us into God's family (v. 16).

Memory Verse

Philemon 16 – "No longer as a slave, but better than a slave, as a dear brother."

Reflection Questions

1. Why does Paul appeal to Philemon "on the basis of love" rather than authority?
2. How does the story of Onesimus demonstrate the transforming power of the gospel?
3. What does Paul's willingness to repay Onesimus's debt teach us about intercession?
4. How does Philemon challenge social divisions in light of Christian brotherhood?
5. How might you apply the principles of reconciliation in your own relationships?

Final Exhortation

Students, Philemon shows us that the gospel is not abstract—it changes how we treat one another. In Christ, enemies become brothers, debts are forgiven, and relationships are restored.

The cross of Christ is the ultimate picture of reconciliation. Just as He paid our debt and welcomed us into God's family, so we are called to forgive, reconcile, and embrace one another in love.

Never underestimate the power of the gospel to transform relationships, communities, and even societies. For in Christ, there is no slave or free, but all are one in Him.

PART IV: THE GENERAL LETTERS

Christ in Faith, Hope, and Love

~ Nineteen ~

HEBREWS

The book of Hebrews is one of the most theologically rich and Christ-centered writings in the New Testament. Its central message is clear: Jesus Christ is greater. Greater than angels, Moses, the priesthood, the law, and the sacrifices of the old covenant.

The unknown author (traditionally linked to Paul but more likely another early church leader) writes to Jewish Christians who were tempted to turn back to Judaism under the weight of persecution. He reminds them that Christ is the fulfillment of all the shadows of the Old Testament. To abandon Him is to abandon the only true salvation.

The heartbeat of Hebrews is this declaration: "But now he has obtained a more excellent ministry, by as much as he is also the mediator of a better covenant, which has been enacted on better promises." (Hebrews 8:6).

Background of Hebrews

- Author: Unknown (possibly Apollos, Barnabas, or Paul).
- Date: ~AD 65–70, before the destruction of the temple.
- Audience: Jewish Christians under persecution, tempted to return to Judaism.
- Purpose: To exalt Christ above all and encourage perseverance in faith.

• Key Verse: "Let us fix our eyes on Jesus, the author and perfecter of our faith." (Hebrews 12:2).

Structure of Hebrews

1. The Supremacy of Christ (Ch. 1–4)
   ◦ Greater than angels.
   ◦ Greater than Moses.
2. The Priesthood of Christ (Ch. 5–10)
   ◦ A better priesthood (after the order of Melchizedek).
   ◦ A better covenant.
   ◦ A better sacrifice.
3. The Call to Persevere (Ch. 11–13)
   ◦ Examples of faith (ch. 11).
   ◦ Run with endurance (ch. 12).
   ◦ Practical exhortations (ch. 13).

Key Themes of Hebrews

1. Christ's Supremacy – He is greater than all who came before.
2. The Better Covenant – Built on better promises.
3. Christ's High Priesthood – He intercedes eternally for us.
4. Faith and Perseverance – Do not turn back—press forward.
5. The Finality of Christ's Sacrifice – Once for all, sufficient forever.

Exposition and Lessons

1. Christ Greater Than Angels and Moses (Ch. 1–4)

Jesus is the radiance of God's glory and the exact representation of His being. He is greater than angels and Moses, the greatest figures in Judaism. Therefore, His message demands obedience.

Lesson: To reject Christ is to reject God's ultimate revelation.

2. The Great High Priest (Ch. 5–7)

Unlike the priests of the old covenant, Jesus is a perfect and eternal High Priest, after the order of Melchizedek. He sympathizes with our weaknesses and intercedes for us.

Lesson: Christ's priesthood guarantees access to God and eternal salvation.

3. The Better Covenant (Ch. 8–10)

The old covenant was a shadow, pointing to Christ. He mediates a better covenant, sealed by His blood, offering forgiveness once for all. His sacrifice is superior to animal sacrifices, which could never take away sin.

Lesson: Christ's work is final and sufficient—there is no need for any other sacrifice.

4. The Heroes of Faith (Ch. 11)

Hebrews 11 recounts the "Hall of Faith," from Abel to Abraham to Moses. These saints endured trials by faith, yet they awaited the fulfillment that we now have in Christ.

Lesson: Faith endures by trusting in God's promises even without immediate results.

5. Run the Race with Endurance (Ch. 12)

Since we are surrounded by this great cloud of witnesses, we must run with perseverance, fixing our eyes on Jesus, who endured the cross for the joy set before Him.

Lesson: Perseverance flows from focusing on Christ, not our circumstances.

6. Final Exhortations (Ch. 13)

The letter closes with practical instructions: love one another, honor marriage, avoid greed, respect leaders, and continually offer praise to God.

Lesson: Faith in Christ must be lived out in daily obedience.

Christ Revealed in Hebrews

- The Radiance of God's glory (1:3).
- The Greater Moses (3:3).
- The Great High Priest (4:14–16).
- The Mediator of a Better Covenant (8:6).
- The Perfect Sacrifice, once for all (10:12).
- The Author and Perfecter of our Faith (12:2).

Memory Verse

Hebrews 12:2 – "Let us fix our eyes on Jesus, the author and perfecter of our faith."

Reflection Questions

1. Why does Hebrews emphasize that Jesus is greater than angels, Moses, and the old covenant?
2. What does it mean that Jesus is our Great High Priest?
3. How does Hebrews 11 inspire perseverance in faith?
4. Why is Christ's sacrifice "once for all" so important for our assurance?
5. How can we "run with endurance" in our daily Christian walk?

Final Exhortation

Students, Hebrews lifts our eyes to see the greatness of Christ. Do not turn back to old ways, religious rituals, or worldly comforts. Christ is enough—greater than anything the world or religion can offer.

When trials press in, fix your eyes on Jesus. When faith feels weak, remember the witnesses who endured before you. And when sin weighs heavy, rest in the sufficiency of Christ's sacrifice.

Stand firm, endure with faith, and run your race with eyes on the One who has already finished it for you.

~ Twenty ~

JAMES

The book of James is one of the most practical writings in the New Testament. While Paul often emphasizes that we are justified by faith apart from works, James emphasizes that genuine faith produces works. These are not in contradiction but in harmony: Paul addresses how we are saved, while James describes how the saved live.

James, the half-brother of Jesus and leader of the Jerusalem church, writes to scattered believers facing trials and temptations. His message is straightforward, at times sharp: faith without works is dead.

The heartbeat of James is found in "Do not merely listen to the word, and so deceive yourselves. Do what it says." (James 1:22).

Background of James

- Author: James, the brother of Jesus and leader of the Jerusalem church.
- Date: ~AD 45–50, making it one of the earliest New Testament writings.
- Audience: Jewish Christians scattered by persecution.
- Purpose: To call believers to authentic faith expressed in godly living.
- Key Verse: "Faith by itself, if it is not accompanied by action, is dead." (James 2:17).

Structure of James

1. Faith Tested by Trials (Ch. 1)
   - Joy in trials.
   - Hearing and doing the Word.
2. Faith and Works (Ch. 2)
   - Rejecting favoritism.
   - Faith proven by deeds.
3. Faithful Speech (Ch. 3)
   - Controlling the tongue.
   - True wisdom from above.
4. Faith and Humility (Ch. 4)
   - Warning against worldliness.
   - Submitting to God.
5. Faith and Perseverance (Ch. 5)
   - Warning to the rich oppressors.
   - Patience in suffering.
   - Power of prayer.

Key Themes of James

1. Faith in Action – True faith shows itself in works.
2. Endurance in Trials – Testing produces maturity.
3. The Power of Words – The tongue reveals the heart.
4. Wisdom from Above – Pure, peace-loving, considerate, submissive.
5. Prayer and Perseverance – The righteous prayer is powerful.

Exposition and Lessons

1. Trials and Maturity (Ch. 1)

James urges believers to count trials as joy, because they produce perseverance and maturity. He warns against hearing without doing the Word.

Lesson: Trials refine faith, and obedience proves it.

2. Faith and Works (Ch. 2)

James confronts favoritism in the church and declares that faith without works is dead. Even demons believe, but saving faith is shown through obedience.

Lesson: Genuine faith results in action—caring for the poor, obeying God, serving others.

3. The Tongue and Wisdom (Ch. 3)

James warns that the tongue is small but powerful, capable of great harm. True wisdom is not jealous or selfish but pure and peaceable.

Lesson: Words reveal the condition of the heart and must be surrendered to God.

4. Humility Before God (Ch. 4)

James rebukes worldliness, calling believers to submit to God, resist the devil, and draw near to Him. Pride leads to destruction, but humility brings grace.

Lesson: God honors the humble and opposes the proud.

5. *Patience and Prayer (Ch. 5)*

James calls for patience in suffering, pointing to Job as an example. He urges prayer for healing, restoration, and forgiveness, declaring: "The prayer of a righteous person is powerful and effective." (5:16).

Lesson: Prayer is a lifeline in trials and a weapon for spiritual victory.

Christ Revealed in James

- The Lord of glory (2:1).
- The Judge standing at the door (5:9).
- The Healer through prayer and faith (5:15).
- The Source of wisdom from above (3:17).

Memory Verse

James 1:22 – "Do not merely listen to the word, and so deceive yourselves. Do what it says."

Reflection Questions

1. Why does James call believers to count trials as joy?
2. What is the difference between faith that saves and dead faith?
3. How do our words reveal our inner spiritual condition?
4. Why is humility essential in resisting worldliness?
5. How does James encourage believers to persevere in suffering and prayer?

Final Exhortation

Students, James confronts us with the reality that true faith must be visible. It is not enough to profess Christ—we must practice our faith daily in works of obedience, love, humility, and perseverance.

The call of James is urgent and practical: be doers of the Word, not hearers only. Let your trials produce maturity. Let your words reflect Christ. Let your humility invite God's grace. And let your prayers unleash His power.

Faith without works is dead, but faith lived out in action transforms lives and communities. May your faith be alive, vibrant, and fruitful for the glory of Christ.

~ Twenty One ~

1 PETER

The letter of 1 Peter is a message of hope written to suffering believers scattered across Asia Minor. They were experiencing persecution, rejection, and social marginalization because of their faith. Into this context, Peter writes to remind them that they are God's chosen people, called to live as strangers in this world, anchored in the living hope of Christ's resurrection.

Peter's central encouragement is this: "Stand firm in the true grace of God." (1 Peter 5:12).

This letter teaches us how to live faithfully in a hostile world—with holiness, submission, perseverance, and above all, hope.

Background of 1 Peter

- Author: The Apostle Peter.
- Date: ~AD 62–64, likely written from Rome ("Babylon").
- Audience: Believers scattered throughout Asia Minor facing persecution.
- Purpose: To encourage suffering Christians to stand firm in grace.
- Key Verse: "But in your hearts revere Christ as Lord. Always be prepared to give an answer to everyone who asks you to give the reason for the hope that you have." (1 Peter 3:15).

Structure of 1 Peter

1. Hope in Salvation (Ch. 1)
   - New birth into a living hope.
   - Call to holiness.
2. Hope in the Church (Ch. 2)
   - The people of God, a chosen priesthood.
   - Living as strangers in the world.
3. Hope in Submission (Ch. 3)
   - Submission in relationships.
   - Suffering for righteousness' sake.
4. Hope in Suffering (Ch. 4)
   - Sharing in Christ's sufferings.
   - Living for the will of God.
5. Hope in Glory (Ch. 5)
   - Shepherding the flock faithfully.
   - Standing firm in grace.

Key Themes of 1 Peter

1. Living Hope – Grounded in the resurrection of Jesus.
2. Holiness in a Hostile World – God's people set apart.
3. Submission for the Lord's Sake – In society, marriage, and work.
4. Suffering as a Test of Faith – Sharing in Christ's sufferings.
5. Glory to Come – Future reward for faithful endurance.

Exposition and Lessons

1. A Living Hope (Ch. 1)

Peter begins with praise: through Christ's resurrection, believers have new birth into a living hope and an inheritance that can never perish. Trials refine faith like gold in fire.

Lesson: Hope is not wishful thinking but a living reality anchored in Christ.

2. God's Chosen People (Ch. 2)

Believers are living stones being built into a spiritual house. They are chosen, royal, holy, and set apart to declare God's praises.

Lesson: Our identity in Christ shapes how we live in the world.

3. Submission for the Lord's Sake (Ch. 2-3)

Peter calls for submission to authorities, masters, and in marriage—not as weakness but as testimony. Christ's own suffering is the ultimate model.

Lesson: Submission is strength under God's control, pointing others to Christ.

4. Suffering with Christ (Ch. 4)

Peter reframes suffering as participation in Christ's sufferings. Believers should not be surprised at fiery trials but rejoice that they share in Christ's glory.

Lesson: Suffering for Christ is not punishment—it is privilege.

5. Shepherding and Standing Firm (Ch. 5)

Peter exhorts elders to shepherd the flock willingly and humbly. He reminds all believers to be alert, because the devil prowls like a roaring lion. Victory comes by resisting him and standing firm in God's grace.

Lesson: The Christian life is a battle, but grace sustains us to the end.

Christ Revealed in 1 Peter

- The Living Hope through resurrection (1:3).
- The Cornerstone chosen by God (2:6).
- The Suffering Servant who bore our sins (2:24).
- The Example in suffering (2:21).
- The Chief Shepherd who rewards faithfully (5:4).

Memory Verse

1 Peter 3:15 – "But in your hearts revere Christ as Lord. Always be prepared to give an answer... for the hope that you have."

Reflection Questions

1. How does Peter describe the "living hope" believers have in Christ?
2. Why is our identity as God's chosen people so important in a hostile world?
3. What does submission look like in society, marriage, and work according to Peter?
4. How should Christians view suffering for righteousness' sake?
5. How can we stand firm in grace when the enemy attacks?

Final Exhortation

Students, 1 Peter reminds us that suffering is not the end of the story—hope is. The resurrection of Christ guarantees an unshakable inheritance. You are chosen, set apart, and empowered to live holy lives even in a hostile world.

When you suffer, remember you are sharing in Christ's sufferings. When the enemy roars, resist him by standing firm in grace.

And when the world questions your faith, be ready to answer with gentleness and respect.

The grace of God will sustain you, and the glory of Christ will be revealed. Stand firm, beloved, for your hope is alive in Him.

~ Twenty Two ~

2 PETER

The letter of 2 Peter is the apostle's farewell message, written with urgency as his death drew near. His goal was to remind believers of God's promises, warn them about false teachers, and call them to grow in the grace and knowledge of Christ.

Where 1 Peter focuses on hope in suffering, 2 Peter emphasizes truth in the face of deception. It reminds us that spiritual growth is not optional but essential if we are to resist error and remain steadfast until Christ returns.

The heart of 2 Peter is captured in "But grow in the grace and knowledge of our Lord and Savior Jesus Christ. To him be glory both now and forever! Amen." (2 Peter 3:18).

Background of 2 Peter

- Author: The Apostle Peter.
- Date: ~AD 65–68, shortly before Peter's martyrdom in Rome.
- Audience: Believers scattered across Asia Minor.
- Purpose: To stir believers to spiritual growth, warn against false teachers, and remind them of Christ's return.
- Key Verse: "Grow in the grace and knowledge of our Lord and Savior Jesus Christ." (2 Peter 3:18).

Structure of 2 Peter

1. The Call to Spiritual Growth (Ch. 1)
    ◦ God's power gives all we need.
    ◦ Add to faith virtue, knowledge, self-control, persever-
    ance, godliness, brotherly affection, and love.
2. Warning Against False Teachers (Ch. 2)
    ◦ Description of false teachers.
    ◦ Their destructive ways and judgment.
3. The Certainty of Christ's Return (Ch. 3)
    ◦ Scoffers deny His coming.
    ◦ The Day of the Lord will come.
    ◦ Living in holy anticipation.

Key Themes of 2 Peter

1. Spiritual Growth – Believers must pursue maturity in Christ.
2. False Teachers Exposed – Their greed, sensuality, and destruction.
3. God's Judgment and Deliverance – Examples from Noah and
   Lot.
4. The Day of the Lord – The certainty of Christ's return.
5. Perseverance in Truth – Holding fast to apostolic teaching.

Exposition and Lessons

1. Growth in God's Power (Ch. 1)

Peter reminds believers that God's divine power has given
everything needed for life and godliness. He calls them to grow
in virtue, knowledge, and love, making their calling and election
sure.

Lesson: Spiritual growth is evidence of genuine faith.

2. The Authority of Scripture (Ch. 1:16–21)

Peter assures them that his teaching is not a myth—he was an eyewitness of Christ's majesty on the Mount of Transfiguration. He affirms that prophecy comes from God, not human will.

Lesson: God's Word is reliable and authoritative, guiding us in truth.

3. The Danger of False Teachers (Ch. 2)

Peter paints a sobering picture of false teachers: greedy, arrogant, sensual, and exploitative. Like Balaam, they love gain more than truth. Their judgment is certain, but God knows how to rescue the righteous.

Lesson: False teaching is destructive, but God protects His people.

4. Scoffers and the Day of the Lord (Ch. 3)

Scoffers mock the promise of Christ's return, claiming all things remain as they were. Peter insists the Day of the Lord will come like a thief, bringing judgment and renewal. Believers must live in holiness, awaiting the new heavens and new earth.

Lesson: The certainty of Christ's return calls us to holy living today.

5. Growing in Grace (Ch. 3:17–18)

Peter closes by urging believers to guard against error and grow continually in grace and knowledge.

Lesson: Growth is lifelong—no Christian ever "arrives."

Christ Revealed in 2 Peter

- The Glorious Lord revealed on the Mount of Transfiguration (1:16–18).
- The Precious Cornerstone rejected by false teachers.
- The Righteous Judge who will return (3:10).
- The Lord of grace and knowledge (3:18).

Memory Verse

2 Peter 3:18 – "But grow in the grace and knowledge of our Lord and Savior Jesus Christ. To him be glory both now and forever! Amen."

Reflection Questions

1. Why is spiritual growth essential for every believer?
2. How does Peter affirm the authority and reliability of Scripture?
3. What are the characteristics of false teachers described in chapter 2?
4. How does the certainty of Christ's return shape the way we live today?
5. What practical steps can you take to "grow in the grace and knowledge" of Christ?

Final Exhortation

Students, 2 Peter reminds us that the Christian life is a journey of growth. We cannot remain stagnant. To grow is to remain steadfast; to stop growing is to risk drifting.

Guard yourself against false teaching. Anchor yourself in the Word. Live with holy anticipation of Christ's return. And above all, keep growing in the grace and knowledge of Jesus.

This is Peter's final word to the church, and it remains God's word to us: never stop growing in Christ.

~ Twenty Three ~

1 JOHN

The letter of 1 John is a pastoral message of assurance, written by the apostle John, the beloved disciple of Jesus. In an age of false teachings and spiritual confusion, John reminds believers of what true fellowship with God looks like. His focus is simple but profound: truth, obedience, and love.

John writes with fatherly affection, often addressing his readers as "dear children." He wants them to know with certainty that they have eternal life (5:13). In doing so, he provides tests of genuine faith—walking in light, confessing sin, obeying God's commands, and loving one another.

The heart of 1 John is found in his declaration: "God is love. Whoever lives in love lives in God, and God in them." (1 John 4:16).

Background of 1 John

- Author: The Apostle John.
- Date: ~AD 85–95, written from Ephesus.
- Audience: Believers facing Gnostic heresies and doubts about Jesus' identity.
- Purpose: To give assurance of eternal life, warn against false teachers, and call believers to live in love and obedience.
- Key Verse: "I write these things to you who believe... so that you may know that you have eternal life." (1 John 5:13).

Structure of 1 John

1. Walking in the Light (Ch. 1–2)
   - Fellowship with God requires confession of sin and obedience.
2. Tests of True Faith (Ch. 2–3)
   - Obedience to God's commands.
   - Love for one another.
3. Warning Against False Teachers (Ch. 2:18–29; Ch. 4)
   - The spirit of antichrist.
   - Testing the spirits.
4. The Nature of Love (Ch. 4)
   - God is love.
   - Perfect love drives out fear.
5. Assurance of Eternal Life (Ch. 5)
   - Faith in Christ as the Son of God.
   - Victory through faith.

Key Themes of 1 John

1. God is Light – Truth and holiness are in Him.
2. God is Love – His love transforms how we love others.
3. Tests of Genuine Faith – Belief, obedience, and love.
4. Victory in Christ – Overcoming the world by faith.
5. Assurance of Eternal Life – Confidence in salvation.

Exposition and Lessons

1. Walking in the Light (Ch. 1)

John declares that God is light; in Him is no darkness. Fellowship with Him requires confession of sin, not denial. The blood of Jesus cleanses us from all sin.

Lesson: True fellowship with God requires honesty, humility, and dependence on Christ's cleansing blood.

2. Tests of Faith (Ch. 2–3)

Obedience and love are central to genuine faith. The one who claims to know God but disobeys Him is a liar. The one who hates his brother is still in darkness.

Lesson: Faith that does not produce obedience and love is counterfeit.

3. False Teachers and Antichrists (Ch. 2:18–29; Ch. 4)

John warns of deceivers who deny that Jesus is the Christ. He calls believers to test the spirits, for not every spirit is from God.

Lesson: Sound doctrine matters—truth protects us from deception.

4. The God of Love (Ch. 4)

John emphasizes that love is the defining mark of God's children. Love flows from God, for God is love. Perfect love drives out fear, giving believers confidence on the day of judgment.

Lesson: The love of God, perfected in us, assures us of His presence and casts out fear.

5. Assurance of Eternal Life (Ch. 5)

John closes by affirming that those who believe in the Son of God have eternal life. Faith overcomes the world, and God's testimony about His Son secures our confidence.

Lesson: Assurance is not based on feelings but on God's promises.

Christ Revealed in 1 John

- The Word of Life made manifest (1:1–2).
- The Advocate with the Father (2:1).
- The Atoning Sacrifice for sins (2:2).
- The Son of God who gives eternal life (5:11–12).

Memory Verse

1 John 5:13 – "I write these things to you who believe... so that you may know that you have eternal life."

Reflection Questions

1. What does it mean to "walk in the light" as John describes?
2. How does John test whether faith is genuine or false?
3. Why is love essential to the Christian life?
4. How can believers discern truth from false teaching today?
5. What gives us assurance of eternal life according to John?

Final Exhortation

Students, 1 John is a call to authentic Christianity. The world is full of falsehood and confusion, but those who walk in light, love in truth, and hold fast to Christ can live with confidence.

You can know that you belong to Him. You can live without fear, because His perfect love casts out fear. And you can rest in the assurance that eternal life is yours in Christ Jesus.

So walk in the light, live in love, reject deception, and rejoice in the victory that overcomes the world—our faith in Christ.

~ Twenty Four ~

2 JOHN

The letter of 2 John is short—just thirteen verses—but it delivers a powerful message about the balance of truth and love. Written by the apostle John, this epistle warns against false teachers who deny the truth about Jesus Christ, while urging believers to walk in love.

In a world full of deception, John reminds us that truth without love becomes harsh, but love without truth becomes weak. Both must be held together for the church to remain faithful.

The heart of 2 John is captured in "It has given me great joy to find some of your children walking in the truth, just as the Father commanded us." (2 John 4).

Background of 2 John

- Author: The Apostle John.
- Date: ~AD 85–95, late in John's life.
- Audience: "The elect lady and her children" (likely a local church and its members).
- Purpose: To exhort believers to walk in truth and love while rejecting false teachers.
- Key Verse: "Walk in the truth, just as we have been commanded by the Father." (2 John 4).

Structure of 2 John

1. Greeting and Joy (v. 1–4)
   - Rejoicing that believers are walking in truth.
2. Command to Love (v. 5–6)
   - Love is obeying God's commands.
3. Warning Against Deceivers (v. 7–11)
   - Many deceivers deny Jesus Christ came in the flesh.
   - Do not welcome false teachers.
4. Final Words (v. 12–13)
   - Desire to meet face-to-face.
   - Closing greetings.

Key Themes of 2 John

1. Truth and Love – Both must be held together.
2. Obedience to God's Commands – Love is expressed in obedience.
3. Warning Against False Teachers – Protecting the church from deception.
4. Discernment in Fellowship – Guarding against partnering with error.
5. Faithfulness in the Basics – Walking daily in what God has already revealed.

Exposition and Lessons

1. Joy in Truth (v. 1–4)

John rejoices that some believers are walking faithfully in truth. Truth is not subjective—it is God's eternal standard.

Lesson: True joy comes when believers live according to God's truth.

2. Love as Obedience (v. 5–6)

John defines love not as mere emotion but as obedience to God's commands. Love and truth are inseparable.

Lesson: Love is proved by action, rooted in God's truth.

3. Warning Against Deceivers (v. 7–11)

John warns of false teachers—those who deny that Jesus came in the flesh. He urges believers not to welcome or support them, for to do so would share in their wicked work.

Lesson: The church must be discerning; fellowship must not compromise truth.

4. Face-to-Face Fellowship (v. 12–13)

John expresses his desire to meet in person, showing the importance of genuine Christian fellowship beyond written words.

Lesson: Technology and letters are valuable, but face-to-face fellowship strengthens the body.

Christ Revealed in 2 John

- The Incarnate One who came in the flesh (v. 7).
- The Truth in whom we walk (v. 4).
- The Commandment of love embodied in Christ (v. 5–6).

Memory Verse

2 John 6 – "And this is love: that we walk in obedience to his commands. As you have heard from the beginning, his command is that you walk in love."

Reflection Questions

1. Why are truth and love inseparable in the Christian life?
2. How does John define love in this short letter?
3. Why does John warn so strongly against welcoming false teachers?
4. What role does discernment play in Christian fellowship to-day?
5. How can we walk in truth and love in a culture of confusion?

Final Exhortation

Students, 2 John reminds us that truth and love must never be separated. A church that has love but no truth loses its foundation, while a church that has truth but no love loses its heart. Both are essential for authentic Christianity.

Guard yourself against deception. Hold fast to the truth about Christ. And walk daily in love, for love fulfills God's commands.

Let your life be a living testimony of both truth and love, so that the world may see Christ in you

~ Twenty Five ~

3 JOHN

The letter of 3 John is the shortest book in the New Testament, yet it delivers a rich lesson on hospitality, truth, and humility in leadership. Unlike 2 John, which warns against receiving false teachers, 3 John encourages believers to support and welcome true ministers of the gospel.

At the same time, John confronts the destructive pride of Diotrephes, who rejected apostolic authority and refused to welcome faithful servants. In contrast, Gaius is commended as a model of faithfulness and hospitality.

The central message of 3 John is this: "Dear friend, you are faithful in what you are doing for the brothers and sisters, even though they are strangers to you." (3 John 5).

Background of 3 John

- Author: The Apostle John.
- Date: ~AD 85–95.
- Audience: Gaius, a faithful believer in a local church.
- Purpose: To commend Gaius for hospitality, warn against Diotrephes, and encourage support of gospel workers.
- Key Verse: "Dear friend, do not imitate what is evil but what is good." (3 John 11).

Structure of 3 John

1. Commendation of Gaius (v. 1–8)
   - Walking in truth.
   - Hospitality to gospel workers.
2. Condemnation of Diotrephes (v. 9–10)
   - Pride, rejection, and opposition.
3. Commendation of Demetrius (v. 11–12)
   - Good testimony from all.
4. Closing Greetings (v. 13–15)

Key Themes of 3 John

1. Walking in the Truth – Faithful living honors God.
2. Hospitality to Gospel Workers – Supporting missions and ministry.
3. Warning Against Pride – The destructive example of Diotrephes.
4. The Power of a Good Testimony – Demetrius as a model of faithfulness.
5. Imitating Good, Not Evil – Following examples of righteousness.

Exposition and Lessons

1. Gaius Commended (v. 1–8)

John rejoices that Gaius is walking in truth and showing hospitality to traveling teachers of the gospel. Supporting them makes Gaius a partner in the work of truth.

Lesson: Hospitality is a vital ministry that advances the gospel.

2. Diotrephes Rebuked (v. 9-10)

John exposes Diotrephes as prideful and controlling. He rejects apostolic authority, spreads malicious gossip, and refuses to welcome faithful workers.

Lesson: Prideful leadership harms the church and opposes Christ.

3. Demetrius Approved (v. 11-12)

John commends Demetrius, whose testimony is confirmed by everyone. He serves as a positive example for others to imitate.

Lesson: A good testimony is a powerful witness in the church and world.

4. Final Greetings (v. 13-15)

John closes warmly, expressing his desire for face-to-face fellowship.

Lesson: Christian fellowship is relational and personal, not just doctrinal.

Christ Revealed in 3 John

- The Truth in whom believers walk (v. 3-4).
- The Lord served through hospitality to His people (v. 8).
- The Righteous Judge who opposes pride and honors humility (implied in contrast between Diotrephes and Gaius).

Memory Verse

3 John 11 – "Dear friend, do not imitate what is evil but what is good."

Reflection Questions

1. How did Gaius demonstrate faithfulness and truth in his life?
2. Why is hospitality to gospel workers so important for the mission of the church?
3. What dangers does Diotrephes represent for church leadership today?
4. How does Demetrius provide a positive example of faithfulness?
5. What does John mean when he urges believers to "imitate what is good"?

Final Exhortation

Students, 3 John reminds us that faithfulness is shown not only in doctrine but in deeds. Hospitality to God's servants is an eternal investment, making us partners in the gospel.

At the same time, this letter warns against prideful, self-serving leadership like that of Diotrephes. Such attitudes destroy fellowship and hinder mission. Instead, follow the example of Gaius and Demetrius—live in truth, walk in love, and serve humbly.

The call of 3 John is simple yet profound: imitate what is good. In doing so, you reflect Christ and advance His kingdom.

~ Twenty Six ~

JUDE

The letter of Jude is a brief but urgent call to contend for the faith. Written by Jude, the half-brother of Jesus, this epistle warns believers about false teachers who had secretly infiltrated the church. These deceivers twisted God's grace into license for immorality and denied the authority of Jesus Christ.

Though short, Jude's letter is packed with vivid warnings, Old Testament examples, and a strong exhortation to stand firm. He reminds us that faith is not something we invent—it is something delivered once for all to God's people. Our task is to guard it, live it, and hand it on faithfully.

The heart of Jude's message is found in "Dear friends, although I was very eager to write to you about the salvation we share, I felt compelled to write and urge you to contend for the faith that was once for all entrusted to God's holy people." (Jude 3).

Background of Jude

- Author: Jude, the brother of James and half-brother of Jesus.
- Date: ~AD 65–80.
- Audience: Believers threatened by false teachers within the church.
- Purpose: To warn against false teaching and encourage believers to remain faithful.

• Key Verse: "Contend for the faith that was once for all entrusted to God's holy people." (Jude 3).

Structure of Jude

1. Introduction and Purpose (v. 1–4)
   ◦ Called, loved, and kept by God.
   ◦ Urgent call to contend for the faith.
2. Examples of Judgment (v. 5–16)
   ◦ Israel in unbelief.
   ◦ Fallen angels.
   ◦ Sodom and Gomorrah.
   ◦ Woes upon false teachers.
3. Exhortations to Believers (v. 17–23)
   ◦ Remember the apostles' warnings.
   ◦ Build yourselves up in faith.
   ◦ Keep yourselves in God's love.
   ◦ Show mercy to others.
4. Doxology (v. 24–25)
   ◦ God's ability to keep us from stumbling.
   ◦ Praise to the only God our Savior.

Key Themes of Jude

1. Contending for the Faith – Guarding the truth entrusted to the church.
2. Judgment on False Teachers – God's justice is certain.
3. Living in God's Love – Building up faith and praying in the Spirit.
4. Mercy and Discernment – Restoring others gently while rejecting sin.
5. God's Preserving Power – He is able to keep us from falling.

Exposition and Lessons

1. The Call to Contend (v. 1–4)

Jude begins by reminding believers of their identity: called, loved, and kept. Then he issues his urgent call—contend for the faith, for false teachers are perverting grace.

Lesson: The faith is precious, and we must guard it against distortion.

2. Warnings Through Examples (v. 5–16)

Jude recalls God's past judgments—Israel's unbelief, fallen angels, Sodom's sin, and rebellious figures like Cain, Balaam, and Korah. He compares false teachers to clouds without rain, autumn trees without fruit, wild waves, and wandering stars.

Lesson: False teachers may look impressive but are empty and destined for judgment.

3. Exhortations for Believers (v. 17–23)

Jude urges believers to remember the apostles' warnings about scoffers. Instead of panicking, they are to build themselves up in faith, pray in the Spirit, keep themselves in God's love, and wait for Christ's mercy. They must also show mercy—rescuing the doubting and confronting sin with discernment.

Lesson: In times of deception, the church must be rooted in prayer, faith, and love.

4. The Doxology (v. 24–25)

Jude closes with one of the most powerful doxologies in Scripture: God is able to keep believers from stumbling and present them faultless in glory with great joy.

Lesson: Our security is not in our strength but in God's preserving power.

Christ Revealed in Jude

- The Lord who delivered His people from Egypt (v. 5).
- The Master denied by false teachers (v. 4).
- The Coming Judge with His holy ones (v. 14–15).
- The One who keeps us from falling and presents us in glory (v. 24).

Memory Verse

Jude 24–25 – "To him who is able to keep you from stumbling and to present you before his glorious presence without fault and with great joy—to the only God our Savior be glory, majesty, power and authority, through Jesus Christ our Lord, before all ages, now and forevermore! Amen."

Reflection Questions

1. What does it mean to "contend for the faith" in your life and ministry?
2. How do the Old Testament examples highlight God's judgment on sin?
3. What dangers do false teachers pose to the church today?
4. How can believers build themselves up in faith and keep themselves in God's love?
5. How does the doxology in verses 24–25 strengthen your confidence in God?

Final Exhortation

Students, Jude calls us to vigilance. The faith we hold is not ours to reshape—it was delivered once for all to the saints. Our task is to guard it, live it, and hand it on faithfully.

Do not be intimidated by false teachers or shaken by scoffers. Build your life on God's Word, pray in the Spirit, and stay in His love. And remember this: your security rests not in your strength but in the God who is able to keep you from stumbling and present you faultless in glory.

Let us contend for the faith with courage and humility, trusting in the One who has already won the victory.

PART V: THE REVELATION

Christ in His Glory

~ Twenty Seven ~

REVELATION

Super In-Depth Expository

No book unveils the supremacy of Jesus more completely than Revelation. It is not chiefly "about beasts and bowls," but—as its opening line declares—"the revelation of Jesus Christ" (Rev 1:1). Here we behold the risen, reigning, returning Lord in glory: the Faithful Witness, Firstborn from the Dead, Ruler of the Kings of the Earth (1:5), the Alpha and Omega (1:8), the Lion who is a Lamb (5:5-6), the Word of God who rides forth (19:13), and the Bridegroom who makes all things new (21:5).

Revelation does not invite speculation so much as adoration and perseverance. It forms resilient disciples who resist compromise, worship Christ above all powers, and live in hope as they suffer. Read it to see Jesus—and seeing Him, overcome (12:11).

Background & How to Read Revelation

- Author: John (the apostle), exiled on Patmos (1:1, 1:9).
- Date/Setting: c. AD 95, during Roman pressure on the churches of Asia.

- Genre: A prophecy (1:3), cast in apocalyptic symbols, delivered as a pastoral letter to seven real congregations (1:4; chs. 2–3).
- Reading posture:
  - Christ-centered: Every scene unveils who Jesus is and what He does.
  - Symbol-aware: Numbers/colors/creatures are rich with Old Testament echoes (e.g., Exodus plagues, Daniel's beasts, Ezekiel's temple, Isaiah's new creation).
  - Pastoral/ethical: The point is endurance and holiness, not a secret calendar.
  - Pattern & cycles: Judgments (seals, trumpets, bowls) intensify and recapitulate the same age-long conflict, culminating in final victory.

Key Verse: "Do not be afraid. I am the First and the Last. I am the Living One; I was dead, and now look, I am alive for ever and ever!" (Rev 1:17–18)

Big-Picture Flow

1. Prologue & Vision of the Son of Man (Ch. 1)
2. Christ's Letters to the Seven Churches (Chs. 2–3)
3. Throne Room & the Slain-Yet-Standing Lamb (Chs. 4–5)
4. Seals: Suffering, Witness, and Safety in the Lamb (Chs. 6–7)
5. Trumpets: Warning Judgments & the Two Witnesses (Chs. 8–11)
6. The Dragon, the Beasts, and the Lamb's People (Chs. 12–14)
7. Bowls: Final Judgments & Fall of Babylon (Chs. 15–18)
8. Hallelujah! The Wedding & the Warrior-King (Ch. 19)
9. Defeat of the Dragon, Final Judgment (Ch. 20)
10. New Heavens, New Earth, New Jerusalem (Chs. 21–22)

Exposition & Life-Lessons

1) The Son of Man among His Churches (1:9–20)

John, suffering "on account of the word of God", meets the glorified Christ. Eyes like fire, voice like many waters, face like the sun—Jesus walks among His lampstands (churches), holding their messengers in His hand.

Lesson: The church is not orphaned. Christ is present, aware, and authoritative in every season.

2) Seven Letters: Christ's Pastoral Assessment (2–3)

To Ephesus, Smyrna, Pergamum, Thyatira, Sardis, Philadelphia, Laodicea: each message follows a pattern—Christ revealed → commendation → correction → call to conquer → promise.

- Ephesus: Orthodox but loveless—return to first love.
- Smyrna: Poor yet rich—be faithful unto death.
- Pergamum/Thyatira: Resist compromise with idolatry/immorality.
- Sardis: Reputation without life—wake up!
- Philadelphia: Little power, great faith—hold fast.
- Laodicea: Lukewarm self-reliance—open the door to the knocking King.

Lesson: Christ cares about truth, love, purity, endurance, authenticity. Overcomers receive crowns, hidden manna, white garments, a new name.

3) The Throne, the Scroll, and the Only Worthy One (4–5)

Heaven opens. Chapter 4: God on the throne—holy, sovereign, worshiped by elders and living creatures. Chapter 5: A sealed scroll (history's plan) awaits a worthy opener. No one qualifies—until the Lion of Judah appears... as a Lamb who was slain yet standing. Heaven erupts: "You were slain, and by your blood you ransomed people for God... and you have made them a kingdom and priests" (5:9–10).

Lesson: The Lamb's sacrifice is the key to history. Power is redefined by the cross; victory comes through self-giving love.

4) The Seals: Suffering Unveiled... and the Sealed Protected (6–7)

The first four seals reveal the horsemen (conquest, war, famine, death)—the brokenness of a fallen age. The martyrs cry, "How long?" The sixth seal shakes creation; the world asks, "Who can stand?" Answer (ch. 7): the sealed servants of God (symbolized by 144,000) and the great multitude from every nation, washed in the Lamb's blood.

Lesson: God does not promise the church escape from all suffering, but He guarantees preservation through it and vindication after it.

5) The Trumpets: Mercy that Warns (8–11)

Trumpets sound partial judgments—warning shots calling the world to repentance. Amid these scenes, the two witnesses (prophetic church) testify, suffer, and are vindicated. The seventh trumpet proclaims: "The kingdom of the world has become the kingdom of our Lord and of His Christ."

Lesson: God's judgments are both just and merciful, designed to wake the rebellious and strengthen the faithful. The church's vocation is witness, even when costly.

6) The Deep Conflict: Dragon, Beasts, and the Lamb's People (12–14)

A panoramic symbolic drama:

- The Woman (God's people) gives birth to the Male Child (Messiah).
- The Dragon (Satan) fails to devour the Child, wages war on the Woman's offspring (the church).
- Two Beasts rise—one of political coercion, one of religious/propaganda deception—demanding allegiance (the infamous "mark").
- In contrast, the 144,000 with the Lamb bear His name—their worship and fidelity distinguish them.

Lesson: Through every age, the enemy weaponizes state power and lying ideologies to counterfeit worship. The church resists by allegiance to the Lamb. The real "mark" to seek is not numbers, but Christ's name written on our lives.

7) The Bowls & Fall of Babylon (15–18)

Seven bowls pour out final, comprehensive judgments. The Great Prostitute, Babylon—symbol of idolatrous wealth, oppression, and seduction—falls. Kings, merchants, and sailors weep; heaven rejoices. Babylon is any system that profits by dehumanizing image-bearers and drugs the nations with luxury and lies.

Lesson: God judges empires that exalt wealth, exploit people, and defy His reign. The church must "come out of her"—reject her values and refuse her compromises.

8) Hallelujah! The Wedding & the Warrior-King (19)

Heaven's Hallelujah chorus celebrates the marriage of the Lamb; the bride (church) wears "fine linen, bright and clean"—the righteous deeds of the saints. Then the Faithful and True rides forth: eyes aflame, many crowns, the Word of God, King of kings and Lord of lords.

Lesson: The story ends not with our fear but with our feast; not with chaos but with covenant joy. Christ's justice is not a threat to the faithful but their hope.

9) The Dragon's Last Defeat & the Final Judgment (20)

Satan is restrained, the saints reign, then the deceiver rallies a final rebellion and is thrown into the lake of fire. The Great White Throne appears; the dead are judged "according to their works." Anyone not in the Book of Life faces the second death.

Lesson: Evil does not end by human progress or policy—it ends by divine judgment. Salvation is by grace; judgment is according to works; both truths magnify the Lamb who saves and the Lord who judges.

and final judgment is

10) All Things New: The Bride, the City, the Presence (21-22)

A new heaven and new earth; New Jerusalem descends—God dwelling with humanity. No temple, for the Lord God and the Lamb are its temple. No sun, for the glory of God gives it light. A river of life flows; the tree of life heals nations. The curse is gone. His servants see His face and reign forever. The book ends with a warning (do not add/remove), a promise ("I am coming soon"), and an invitation: "Let the one who is thirsty come... take the water of life without price."

Lesson: Christian hope is not escape to clouds but resurrection life in a renewed creation with unmediated communion with God.

The Fullness of Jesus Christ in Revelation (Christology at a Glance)

- Alpha & Omega; First & Last (1:8, 17; 22:13) — Eternal, sovereign Lord of time.
- Son of Man (1:13) — Daniel's promised ruler, present with His churches.
- Lion of Judah / Root of David (5:5) — Royal Messiah.
- Lamb Slain yet Standing (5:6) — Victory through sacrificial love.
- Redeemer (5:9–10) — Purchases a multi-ethnic kingdom of priests.
- Shepherd (7:17) — Leads to living waters.
- Word of God (19:13) — Executes just judgment.
- Bridegroom (19:7) — Unites with a purified people.
- Temple & Lamp (21:22–23) — God's presence and radiance among His own.
- Fountain of Life (22:1–2, 17) — Source of eternal joy and healing.

Takeaway: Revelation exalts Jesus as Savior, Shepherd, Sovereign, and Spouse—the fullness of God's glory and grace.

Memory Verses

- Revelation 1:17–18 — "Do not be afraid... I was dead, and now I am alive forever and ever."
- Revelation 21:5 — "Behold, I am making all things new."
- Revelation 22:17 — "Let the one who is thirsty come... take the water of life without price."

Reflection & Discussion

1. How do the seven letters reveal what Jesus values in His churches today?
2. Why is the Lamb (not the Lion alone) central to opening the scroll of history?
3. Where do you see "Babylon's" seductions at work in modern culture—and in your heart?
4. What does it practically mean to overcome by the blood of the Lamb and the word of our testimony (12:11)?
5. How does the vision of new creation reshape Christian mission, ethics, and worship right now?

Final Exhortation

Revelation is a discipleship manual in apocalyptic colors. It teaches you to adore Jesus, resist idolatry, bear faithful witness, and suffer with hope. Do not let the symbols obscure the song: Worthy is the Lamb. Do not let the judgments eclipse the joy: Hallelujah, the Lord God omnipotent reigns. Do not let the beasts intimidate you: the Dragon is doomed. And do not let Babylon's glitter seduce you: the Bridegroom is at the door.

Lift your eyes. The scars in His hands are your guarantee. The throne above history is not vacant. The river is already flowing. Hear the final invitation: "Come." And respond with the church's final prayer: "Amen. Come, Lord Jesus!" (22:20)

Dr. Tony Medley Sr. is a pastor, teacher, mentor, and author whose life and ministry have been dedicated to helping people discover the power of God's Word spoken over their lives. Known for his passionate preaching and practical teaching, Dr. Medley has spent decades equipping believers to hear God's voice, walk in their identity in Christ, and live with purpose and bold faith. His ministry extends beyond the pulpit—through books, training materials, stage plays, and discipleship resources—designed to ignite transformation in individuals, churches, and communities.

Dr. Medley combines deep biblical insight with everyday application, ensuring that readers not only understand the Scriptures but also live them out with confidence. With a message that is both prophetic and practical, Dr. Medley inspires people to see themselves through heaven's perspective. He believes every person is "wrapped in the conversation" of God and destined to thrive in His promises.

When he is not writing or teaching, Dr. Medley is serving his church family, mentoring emerging leaders, and enjoying time with his own family, who remain his greatest earthly joy.